the
Beader's
Workbook

the Beader's Workbook

More than 50 Beading Projects for Jewelry and Accessories

Kathleen Barry

www.fwmedia.com

17   16   15   14   13   5   4   3   2   1

DISTRIBUTED IN CANADA BY FRASER DIRECT
100 Armstrong Avenue
Georgetown, ON, Canada L7G 5S4
Tel: (905) 877-4411

DISTRIBUTED IN THE U.K. AND EUROPE BY F&W MEDIA INTERNATIONAL
Brunel House, Newton Abbot, Devon, TQ12 4PU, England
Tel: (+44) 1626 323200, Fax: (+44) 1626 323319
Email: enquiries@fwmedia.com

DISTRIBUTED IN AUSTRALIA BY CAPRICORN LINK
P.O. Box 704, S. Windsor NSW, 2756 Australia
Tel: (02) 4560 1600, Fax: (02) 4577 5288
E-mail: books@capricornlink.com.au

SRN: U8137
ISBN-13: 978-1-4402-3873-4

This book is dedicated to my son and our family who have all given up so much of their time to help make it possible.

Special thanks to My Mother "Oumatjie" who does all the hard work. My very patient suppliers and friends and to Wilsia who has an extreme sport as a profession.

media

5410 5712
6/14

Originally published by Metz Press
1 Cameronians Avenue
Welgemoed, 7530
South Africa

Copyright © Metz Press 2013
Text copyright © Kathleen Barry
Photographs copyright © Metz Press

Publisher and editor	Wilsia Metz
Design and lay-out	Angie Hausner
Cover design	Geoffrey Raker
Photographer	Ivan Naudé
Reproduction	Color/Fusion, Green Point
Printing and binding	Printed and bound in China by WKT Co Ltd

Contents

Introduction

The idea behind writing this book is to share some of my designs and techniques with fellow beaders and to help potential beaders consolidate the minefield of often confusing technical jargon which gets filtered down through the ranks.

As beading has grown increasingly popular the amount of information available has also increased. Being self taught I only became exposed to this some time after I was fairly accomplished and was therefore able to work through it more easily. Having said that, trial and error is a slow and expensive way of learning things and with our busy lifestyles, it's not many of us that can afford the luxury of lengthy contemplation.

Like beads, beading techniques come in many guises. There is a style of beading for almost everyone, from intricate needle and thread techniques to simply-strung statement pieces with the ultimate impact often determined by the choice of beads and materials rather than the actual technique as such.

The techniques described in this book are referred to in more formal circles as bead stringing which also covers working with wire and chain. The projects range from very simple to quite challenging and have been chosen for versatility and flexibility. I therefore advise you not to try to follow each project too rigidly but to make them your own and to add something of your personality to each one. Trying to match materials exactly can become quite frustrating and denies you the adventure of finding what works best for you. I often find that having to adapt projects slightly would steer me into a new direction with very positive and innovative results.

BEADING AS A HOBBY

This is a very rewarding and therapeutic pastime with many other advantages: no large work area is required, there are no lengthy drying or setting times and you see instant results. I am sure that one of the reasons for its rise in popularity is that you can wear what you make or give it as gifts, so many people are able to notice and admire your talent and skill. This is great fuel for creative inspiration!

BEADING AS A CAREER

If you do beading as a career, my advice is that you should try to cultivate a signature style instead of trying to keep up with the fast moving fashion trends. Blindly following fashion can seriously dent your bead budget and competing with the mass market is not very rewarding. Work towards a dedicated client base – people who appreciate your talent and style. I find it much easier designing a piece for someone I know than mass-producing items. When you buy beads, carefully record the prices so that you are able to price your items accurately even if you only use the beads at a much later stage.

WHAT TO EXPECT FROM SUPPLIERS

Look for a supplier with a good range of beads and findings. Quality is most important, and then price. If you do compare prices, always be sure that you are comparing apples with apples. Do not be shy to ask about the origin of materials. Try to find a supplier who is a hands-on beader. There is nothing more frustrating than not finding what you are looking for and then not getting any assistance from your supplier in your quest to come up with a suitable alternative.

BEAD SHOPPING

Try to shop with a specific project in mind. I find it very hard to design in a bead shop. Until you are quite confident and have a fairly well-stocked bead collection it is better to know exactly what you are going to make before venturing into a bead shop where you may feel overwhelmed at the choice. Make a list or take your book with you. Alternatively you can use an existing piece to work out the number of beads required and what sizes you will need.

BEAD STORAGE

Be very disciplined with this. Try not to rip open the packets and start creating the moment you get home, then waltz off in search of the closest admirer (that's me by the way)! Get several multi-compartment containers and store different kinds of beads together. Or arrange them by colour or size – whatever works for you. It is also useful to have small multi–compartment containers should you need to take beads with you to a class or on holiday.

HOW TO USE THIS BOOK

To assist you in your choice of materials the book kicks off with a brief outline of the main items used for the projects, looking at what is available and giving you some buyer's hints and tips to facilitate your task. One of the attractions of beading is that there is something for everyone, and you are bound to find what appeals to you.

The emphasis then shifts to the basic techniques. I feel that if you dedicate some time to mastering these, it will give you increased creative freedom and executing these projects will be much easier. I am confident that once you are familiar with the basic techniques most of you will be designing your very own masterpieces in no time.

The bulk of the book consists of step by step instructions for specific projects. In this section I refer you to the basic techniques where applicable, rather than repeat the same instructions. Use these design ideas and suggestions to add to your own repertoire.

Be aware that many people and, even more so, many publications are terribly serious about their beading. Keep it light, though – your interpretation of techniques and colour choices may be the birth of a new style or technique and there really are no rules. The only rule is to have lots of fun.

Materials and tools

There is such a wide range of beads and beading material available that beaders are truly spoilt for choice. The secret is knowing how to choose from everything that is available only what you really need and not to end up with heaps of unused items you may eventually discard.

In this section I try to touch on the basics, with some buyer's tips thrown in for good measure.

METAL FINDINGS

These are the small metal components that allow us to link, crimp and fasten things together, available in many different metals and specialised finishes. Use the best quality you can find and afford. In most cases I use sterling silver. Silver and gold-plated components are available, but should not be used in high-friction areas as the plating will wear off quickly. However, fashion also dictates and good quality base–metal components – nickel, gold, brass and copper – are widely used and available in a variety of specialised finishes. My favourite is the antique look. If you can find nickel-free findings, buy them as many people develop skin rashes where findings make contact with the skin.

CLASPS

Fastening options for necklaces and bracelets are a business on their own, and new clasps become available all the time. When deciding which clasp to use for which project, factors to consider are the weight of the beads, who will be opening and closing the clasp (for example, elderly people prefer a magnetic clasp or a toggle clasp to a trigger type clasp), where the clasp will be used and whether it will be possible to operate it (for example, a trigger clasp is not suitable for a bracelet as it is difficult for the wearer to open and close with only one hand available – rather use a toggle clasp). Do not be tempted to use a bigger clasp on a delicate necklace with the idea that it will be easier to operate. Such a clasp could be much heavier than all your beadwork and therefore when the necklace is worn the clasp will constantly work its way to the front of the necklace. These are the main types of clasps used for the projects in the book:

Toggle clasps

Used on bracelets and necklaces. A very strong, no-fuss method of fastening, available in many finishes and styles. When fitting, always make sure that the bar end of your clasp and the beads attached to it are able to comfortably pass through the ring end of the clasp. They all need to clear completely before the bar can sit back on the ring in the fastened position. If this does not happen easily the clasp will always be very difficult to open and close successfully.

Pop clasps

Neat and secure; perfect for delicate pieces as there is no pulling on the beadwork to open and close the clasp.

Trigger clasps

Generally a less expensive option, secure and great when using an extension chain. Check that the mechanism is working before you purchase, especially with the antique finishes.

S-clasps

Sometimes difficult to fasten depending on the style, but there is a very large selection available.

Magnetic clasps

Always check the strength of the magnet; some can be very weak and therefore not very effective or secure. These are not recommended for heavy pieces.

Magnetic multi-strand clasps

Useful for multi-strand work, but always check the strength of the magnet and be aware of the magnet strength in relation to the weight of your beads.

CRIMP BEADS

There are many types available, the most secure being precious metal or soft tube crimps that can be folded over. Barrel crimps are good for simple crimping (not folded over) but tend to be quite brittle and sharp.

Crimp covers

These are small seamed beads that are open on one side. After crimping your crimp bead, use a crimp cover by carefully closing it over the squashed crimp for a perfectly neat finish.

Crimp ends

Tube-shaped with a hook and eye attached, cord or leather is fitted inside the tube and then the tube is squashed in the centre with crimping pliers to secure into position.

Thong crimp-ends

An open tube with a loop to attach a ring and a clasp, used with leather thongs and cord. The cord is placed inside the crimp and the two sides are folded over the cord to secure.

Cones and caps

Most commonly used as a neat and decorative cover for multiple beading strands gathered to a central point.

Bead caps

Mostly used as decorative ends for beads, they are also used to prevent pins slipping through beads with large holes. Make sure that they fit the beads that you intend using with them. Rather buy smaller than bigger – you can always use a small bead cap on a large bead, but you cannot use a cap that is too big on a small bead. Some are soft and can be moulded to fit beads with irregular shapes.

3-to-1 connectors

Use these to convert a multi–strand piece to a single-strand, for example when attaching a clasp. These also make great chandelier type earrings

EARRING COMPONENTS

Several kinds are available depending on how they are to be used and whether the earrings are meant for pierced or unpierced ears. Again try to get the best quality available. Nickel-free is a very important criterion. Your choice of earring component depends on the design and the wearer – for a more sophisticated look I always use a ball and post (stud).

Chandelier earring components

These are used to create elaborate earrings with many dangling strands. They can also be used for multi-strand necklaces.

Ear wires and lever backs

These are hooks for pierced ears, with a loop that can be opened and closed for attaching beadwork. Lever backs are hinged and when closed are very secure.

Ball and post components

These are pierced earring studs with a loop for attaching beading. Often these are decorative and they may also be inlaid with gemstones or rhinestones. The back attachments are available with metal or plastic studs.

Clip-on earrings

For wearers who do not have pierced ears you can use a clip-on earring base with a loop that can be opened and closed for adding beadwork.

RINGS

These are used to link various parts of your beadwork and are available in all metal types and finishes. The size will depend on the job that they are intended for. Ensure that you have a good variety of sizes as a too big ring can look very out of place. The quality of rings is very important – if they are too soft your work will keep coming apart.

Jump rings

Most commonly used, these rings can be opened and closed easily and are used for linking items such as charms onto a charm bracelet.

Split rings

Similar to those found on key holders. They cannot be opened unless properly (deliberately) done and are therefore very secure (see basic techniques page 35 for opening instructions).

Perfect rings

These have no seam, therefore thin threads cannot slip through any join. They are often used at the end of a piece so that a clasp can be attached.

PINS

In beadwork these are mostly used to make earrings, beaded charms and links.

Head pins

A flat-ended pin used for beaded charms, earrings etc. In most cases the flat head at one end cannot be pulled through the bead or charm and acts as a stopper. It is used to create a beaded drop, among others, and is closed with a loop on top of the beads (see basic techniques page 34). Available in different lengths and thicknesses, and in different finishes including copper and silver.

Eye pins

Loop-ended pins available in different thicknesses, used for linking beaded loops or chain.

Bails

Attachment for pendants. The most common type is a pinch bail and like the name suggests, you would simply pinch it over the hole in your pendant. The stringing cord is either pushed through an open end in the top of the bail or a loop that is attached to the bail. Check that the bail is big enough to accommodate your pendant.

Sliders

Base-metal components that are both functional and decorative, these can be quite simple or very ornate and often have crystals set into them. Sliders have more than one hole in them, allowing for multiple strands to pass through,

and are used extensively wherever you would like to keep two or more beaded strands apart (in other words, keep the width).

Bali style silver

Sterling silver beads with lots of design detail. They are oxidised (blackened) to accentuate the detail.

Spacer beads

Available in many sizes and designs, I use these to create definition between two different beads, almost like framing the beads. They are also very useful when stringing very large beads together as they allow for movement. Match the metal of your spacers to that of your findings. When using sterling silver I prefer the oxidised spacer beads where the intricate detail is defined.

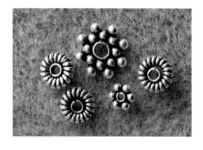

Multi-strand spacers

Much like sliders but not normally as broad, a multi-strand spacer is a thin metal bar with multiple holes for keeping strands apart. Also available in various metals, styles and finishes, some purely functional and plain.

Ring components

A size-adjustable ring base with several beading loops to which beads on pins are attached with common loops.

STRINGING MATERIALS

There are many materials that can be used for stringing beads, many of them traditional and a little outdated. Modern technology has simplified stringing for us with the marvellous invention of flexible beading wire. I do almost all my stringing on this without hesitation. Beading nylon I often use for an invisible look and beading elastic for jewellery with no clasps, that need to be stretched to fit.

Flexible beading wire

This is commonly known as tigertail and consists of multiple strands of thin wire twisted together and sealed with a nylon coating. It can range from seven to 49 (maximim flexibility) strands twisted together and coated, depending on the quality – the more strands the less chance of it kinking permanently. Flexible beading wire is generally very strong and available in many colours including .925 silver. Used in conjunction with crimp beads to secure clasps and so on into place, flexible beading wire has many purposes and can even be used decoratively. It is most commonly found in 0,38 mm (a good allrounder) or 0,45 mm thicknesses, the latter being thicker and therefore suitable for heavier beads.

Beading elastic

This stringing medium is available in many colours and the most commonly available thicknesses range between 0,5 and 1 mm. I find the most versatile is clear beading elastic in 0,7 mm. It is mostly used for elasticated bracelets or jewellery without clasps. Be aware, however, that the elastic loses its elasticity and will perish after some time.

Beading nylon

Also available in a variety of thicknesses and colours. A good all–rounder size is 0,35 mm clear. This is perfect for creating a floating necklace when you do not want a coloured stringing material to detract from the beads. It can be used for basic stringing but is untidy to finish unless crimp beads are used. Be sure to use tube crimps as barrel crimps are sharp edged and may cut the nylon.

Beading wire

Available in precious metal and plated. I mostly use copper-core silver-plated wire if it is in a low friction area, so that the risk of the plating wearing off is minimal. The gauge or thickness used will be determined by the weight of the beads and the technique being used. As a general rule use the thickest wire that you can get to pass through the holes of beads that you are using to be sure that the wire is not too light for the weight of the beads. See basic techniques (page 25) for further details.

Beading cord

You can use cord in any thickness and colour and there is a vast range to choose from. Be aware that waxed cord attracts dirt and therefore has a short lifespan. I mostly use silk cord with a pre–threaded needle. Always make sure that the holes of your beads will allow the cord to pass through when selecting materials for an item using cord.

Leather and suede

I prefer to use the tubular leather as it wears well compared to suede once it has softened. Be sure that you are buying real leather or suede (you can smell if it is leather) as this will be longer lasting. Tubular leather is available in various finishes and colours, even in metallic finishes.

Chain

As with metal findings chain is available in a large range of styles, colours and finishes, normally sold by the metre in a retail bead store. There are no rules with chain and any size can be used to create any effect as trends dictate. Look for good quality chain – you can tell

when looking at the links. If the two ends meet neatly or are soldered, it is safe to assume that it is a well-made chain.

Sterling silver chain

Owing to the nature of silver chain it can be cut as the links are soldered together in most cases and are very secure. I always use sterling silver chain when using other silver findings and beads in a piece.

Metal chain

As with the findings, metal chain is available in many colours and finishes, including antique finish. Choose whatever compliments your beads and be sure to get a good quality. Never cut medium to heavy metal chain with your side cutters – always open a link with two pairs of pliers. If the links are thin or soft, cut the chain.

TOOLS

There are many beading tools that will make your life easier and help you make beaded jewellery with a professional finish. You don't need to buy everything immediately, but a few essential items will get you started. Try to get good quality basic tools as you grow very attached to them. I have replaced all my old tools with professional tools and I am sorry to say that I still prefer the ones I started with.

My recommended basic tools list to get you started would be side cutters, chain-nose pliers (can also be used for simple crimping), round-nose pliers and a crimping tool.

Crimping tool

You can tell a crimping tool from others by the two indentations in the jaw and the very robust handle. It should have a very narrow tip, to allow you to get into small areas between beads. This tool is used specifically to crimp crimping beads correctly in the folded-over way (see basic techniques page 36). Quality is important – the inside teeth of the jaws must be defined and not painted (as this makes it slippery). If you do not have a crimping tool, chain-nose pliers can be used for simple crimping.

Side cutters

These are used to cut wire. Quality is very important and checking that you are buying stainless steel will help to ensure this (they do not have to cost a fortune). When cutting soft wire you should be able to hear a snap.

Round-nose pliers

They look very similar to chain-nose pliers when closed. On opening you will see that they have perfectly rounded jaws inside and are therefore used for all the loop-making techniques with wire, for earrings, pendants and charms. Try to get stainless steel and, very important make sure that the tips of the jaws are aligned when the pliers are closed and viewed from the front.

Chain-nose pliers

They look very similar to round-nose pliers until you open them. You will see that the inside of the jaws is flat, making this tool very useful for gripping things like wire and chain. Chain-nose pliers will be used to hold, open and close loops and components and can also be used for simple crimping. Try to get stainless steel and make sure that the tips of the jaws are aligned when closed. Do not use pliers with ridges – the jaws must be smooth to avoid marking your wire and findings.

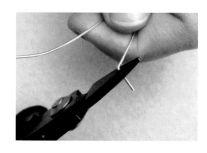

Jump-ring tool

Using this is a smart and easy way to ensure that your rings and loops are being opened correctly without damaging them.

Beading mats

These short-pile mats are usually available in cream, grey and navy blue. I recommend cream or grey as bead colours are distorted on the darker mat. A beading mat is very useful to keep beads from rolling off a work surface. Rest one on a lap tray and you will have a wonderful portable workstation, or as in my case, a few at a time.

Bead reamer

This is a very useful tool with various bit attachments that can be used to enlarge or unblock a hole in a bead. It is mainly used for pearls but used very gently can also file away obstructions in gemstones and glass beads.

BEADS

The range of beads available today is enormous and much like fashion. New and old styles and colours come and go. Many beaders feel quite overwhelmed when faced with such a wide choice. The secret is to try to stay focused on your project at hand. Choose colours that you will wear or that will match a specific outfit if the item you are making is for you. This immediately narrows down your choice and makes the choices more manageable.

In this section I will only highlight some of what is available and give you pointers to bear in mind when next you venture into your favourite bead shop.

Crystals

Crystals have become more readily available over the past years and are very popular with beaders. They are available in a massive range of exquisite colours and in many shapes and sizes combining very easily with just about any beads. The leading manufacturers of high quality crystal are Swarovsky in Austria and Preciosa in the Czech Republic. These lead

crystal beads are machine cut and polished. Their high lead content makes them sparkle more than standard glass beads, but they are also more fragile than standard glass beads.

The more facetted a crystal the more expensive it will be.

Crystal bicones This is the least facetted and therefore least expensive shape. Available in all the colours manufactured. Useful sizes are 4, 5, 6 and 8 mm.

Crystal round shape Useful sizes are 6, 8 and 10 mm.

Crystal cosmic shape A very rewarding if unusual bead as it has a great impact owing to its unique shape and size.

Crystal drop shape Also called a briolette, this is a facetted top-drilled bead that should hang freely for maximum sparkle impact. Sizes vary from supplier to supplier from very small 4/5 mm and up.

Crystal doughnut shape A very versatile, highly facetted crystal often used as a spacer bead. Available in 6 and 8 mm.

Crystal pendants are available in many shapes, colours and sizes and add impact to the simplest piece as a drop.

Drops and briolettes

Top-drilled beads, normally facetted, used extensively in earring and drop or pendant designs. This is quite a challenging shape, and unless you have some good basic techniques behind you I would not recommend these to a beginner beader.

Czech fire-polished beads

These are very good quality facetted glass beads. The shapes and sizes are all uniform and they are therefore very easy to work with. These beads are often incorrectly sold as crystal as they are facetted and similar in shape and style. They do not contain lead and therefore do not sparkle in the same way as crystals do.

Czech pressed glass

Beautiful quality beads available in an enormous range of shapes, sizes and colours and finishes. They always add a special touch to any piece.

Gemstones

Gemstone beads are available in many interesting shapes and colours and are very rewarding to work with. Facetted stones have a great lustre, but the quality of available beads vary considerably. There are also many imitations flooding the market. A sure way to check authenticity is to check the weight and temperature. Real stone is heavy and very cold to the touch.

Gemstones can be bought in many different sizes. In this picture you can see citrine chips (yellow), rose quartz nuggets (pink), matt agate (multi-coloured), mukite (maroon), kainite (blue), blue lace agate (cornflower blue), smokey quartz and clear quartz (back).

The deep orange beads are Carnelian, the black round beads are onyx and the facetted gunmetal beads are hematite (a typical example of a copy of this is hematine).

The pink stones are rose quartz, the clear stones are quartz crystal, the purple stones are amethyst, the soft blue stones are blue topaz. Be aware when buying stones on strands like this string of blue topaz that the thread on which they are strung affects the colour you see. You will note that the blue thread greatly enhances the colour of the beads. Once taken off the strand I can assure you they will be a lot less blue.

Seed beads

These very small beads are used extensively in needle and thread beadwork. I have, however, found many uses for them in stringing as spacers and enjoy their large variety of colours and finishes. They are manufactured mainly in China, India, the Czech Republic and Japan with the highest quality coming from Japan.

Because they are so small, their sizes are indicated as 6° or 11°, indicating how many beads of that size equal nought. The bigger the number, the smaller the bead.

Acrylic beads

Good quality acrylic beads can be identified by the sharpness of their facets and the clarity of the plastic. There is an enormous range available in every imagineable colour and shape. To the untrained eye these are sometimes hard to tell apart from glass. An inexpensive price in relation to the size of the bead, and a light weight are good indicators that you are looking at an acrylic bead.

Lampwork

This is an artform in itself, practised since ancient times. It originated in Murano, Italy in the 1300s, and spread from there to the rest of Europe. Lampwork

beads consist of molten glass and are layered from glass rods under a torch flame to create depth and texture. Now extensively made in China and India lampwork beads have become very popular and more affordable.

Venetian glass beads

Very high quality beads imported from Italy. These are often used sparingly in designs as a focal bead owing to the price. For maximum impact, less is more when using these beads.

Foil glass beads

Copies of Venetian style glass beads, these shown have been made in China and are commonly referred to as foil glass beads.

Facetted glass beads

These beads have more sparkle and depth than smooth beads and can add a lot of life or movement to a design.

Furnace glass beads

Italian glass-blowing techniques have been adapted to make these beads. Furnace glass uses large decorated canes built up out of smaller canes encased in clear glass and then extruded to form the beads with lines and twisting stripes. These beads require a glass furnace for manufacture, hence the name.

Metallised plastic beads

A great, useful product that gives a chunky metal look without adding too much weight. These beads are acrylic with a very thin plating of metal.

Wooden beads

Available in all shapes and sizes, stained, natural, carved, painted, these beads are versatile and add an ethnic feel to designs.

Wire-coil beads

Fun beads that can have smaller beads or charms inserted into them by opening the coils. These are available in several finishes.

Chevron beads

Originaly made in Italy, chevron and rosetta/star beads are now also being manufactured in India and in China. They are very popular collectors' items and are still highly valued in present day West Africa, where they continue to be worn for prestige and ceremonial purposes.

Glass pearls or faux pearls

These beads have been coated with a pearlised finish and are easy to identify by their perfect shape and finish. The best way to tell if they are a fairly good quality is to check that there is no flaking of the outer coating at the holes of the beads.

Freshwater pearls

Freshwater pearls are the most common type of pearl. Their unique shapes and wide variety of colours, combined with their attractive prices, make them accessible to many beaders. Freshwater pearls are best known for their whimsical shapes and wide variety of sizes ranging from tiny seed pearls measuring 1 or 2 mm in diameter to giant pearls of 15 mm and larger. The quality of a pearl is measured by its regularity in shape and its lustre.

Basic techniques

In beading there are several basic techniques which, once you have mastered them, enable you to make just about any piece of jewellery you can think of.

KNOTS
Half hitch (common knot)

1. Make a loop.

2. Take the thread back and through the loop

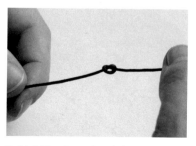

3. Hold both ends of the thread while gently tightening the knot.

Square knot (reef knot)

1. Right over left

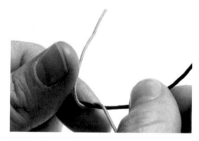

2. Under and up

3. Left over right

4. Under and up

5. Pull tight.

Wire work

Once you have mastered basic wire-work techniques you can do all the projects in this book. I find that precious-metal wire or copper-core beading wire, plated in whichever finish you require, is the most versatile.

Loops

All loops require practice but they are definitely worth mastering and once you have your technique right you can work on your speed. In no time at all you will be wondering what all the fuss was about. Practise making loops with bigger beads (8 mm and up) so that you have something substantial to hold on to, and use soft pins or plated wire with copper core which gives good results and is easy on the hands.

Common loops (or eyes)

Use head pins or wire to make common loops or eyes. The gauge or thickness of your wire will be determined by the weight of your beads: heavier beads require heavier wire. As a general rule I never use less than 0,6 mm (22 gauge) for common loops. **Tools required:** Round-nose pliers and cutters.

1 Thread a bead that needs to have a loop onto a head pin.

2 Bend the tail that is protruding from the bead against the bead at right angles either with your thumb or grasp the tip with round-nose pliers and pull down into position.

3 Cut the wire, leaving a tail just short of 1 cm (9,9 mm) above the bead.

4 Grip the very tip of the wire with round-nose pliers. The position of your pliers determines the size of your loop. I use the very tip of my pliers to get the smallest possible loops.

5 In a fluid motion, curl or rotate the wire into a loop towards the bead as far as your wrist will turn. Release the pliers.

6 Reposition your hand on the pliers to allow you to continue turning at the same place that you left off; keep turning to close the loop.

7 If your loop is not perfectly closed pinch both ends of the base of the bead using the middle section of your round-nose pliers until they meet.

TIP

If you cannot close the loop your original tail in step 3 is being cut too short or your round-nose pliers may be too big. Check that you are positioning them on the tip before you replace them.

8 Straighten the loop if it is leaning over slightly by bending it in the opposite direction to 'pick up its head'.

TIP

To avoid leaning loops, ensure that the original tail is bent over far enough (step 2) and that the tail in step 3 is not left too long.

Connecting loops

Tools required: Chain-nose pliers or standard pliers (no teeth as this will mark your wire).

1 Where the two ends of the loop meet at the base of the bead, gently twist the open end towards you.

2 The opening should be just enough to allow whatever needs to be attached to this loop to slip into the loop.

3 Gently push open end back to close the loop.

Wrapped loops

Soft copper-core plated wire works best. The gauge or thickness of your wire will be determined by the weight of your beads and the size of their holes. I use wrapped loops in many instances when pearls or gemstones have small or irregular holes. Heavier beads will require heavier wire. As a general rule I use at least 0,4 mm for wrapped loops, but seldom heavier than 0,6 mm (22 gauge). Wrapped loops are far more secure than common loops as they will not open when pulled. Expect to make quite a few

wrapped loops before you will make consistently good ones. Use a few handfuls of your left over odd beads and link them with wrapped loops in no particular order to practise – you may be surprised with the result yourself. **Tools required:** Round-nose pliers and cutters.

TIP

Once you are satisfied with the quality of your loops, make a mark on your round-nose pliers with a metal file or something similar at the exact point that you wrap your loop to ensure that your holes are the same size every time.

1 Using a 50 mm piece of wire, wrap the wire around the round-nose pliers like a hairpin leaving a longer (about 30 mm) and shorter end (about 20 mm).

2 Rotate the pliers so that the empty jaw is above the partial loop and continue moving the shorter end of wire around the longer one by pushing it away from you with your thumb ...

3 and bringing it towards you with your index finger.

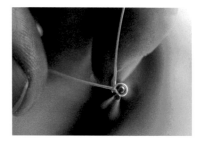

4 Continue in this way to wrap loops around the longer end allowing the coils to form neatly under each other. The number of loops is optional but make at least two to ensure that it will not pull loose.

5 If the loops are sitting slightly away from each other and you prefer them close together like I do, use your thumb nail or Chain–nose pliers to push them upwards towards the newly formed loop and together, taking care not to leave marks on the loops.

6 Trim using the flat side of your cutters, cutting as close to the remaining tail of the coil as you can.

7 Add your bead that will become part of the beaded loop.

8 Begin forming a loop on the other end of the bead, taking care to allow enough space for the coils.

9 Wrap the coils neatly around the wire protruding from the bead, taking the coils as close to the bead as possible.

10 If the loop is slightly tilted gently straighten it with round-nose pliers. This may create space for one more coil to be tucked in at the base of the loop. (Keep this in mind when allowing space for further loops.)

11 Trim the unwanted wire as before. Apply the Sulcas technique to all loops if you have a small wire tail protruding after the cut.

Connecting wrapped loops

1 Repeat steps 1 and 2 of wrapped loops. Before wrapping the loop closed, slip on whatever needs to be attached to the loop (another beaded loop, chain, clasp etc.

2 Remove the pliers and grip the loop on the outside just above the point where the two wires cross to avoid it losing its round shape.

3 Continue to wrap the loop closed as in step 9 of wrapped loops, and trim the excess wire.

4 If you are connecting beaded loops, add another bead at this point. Close with a wrapped loop as described in step 8 of wrapped loops.

The Sulcas technique

Using your crimping tool clamp the indent closest to the tip around your wrapped loop to neatly shape the wire coils.

Beading pins

If you are making jewellery as a business or want to reduce costs, mastering these techniques will be invaluable as good quality pins can inflate material costs in a piece using a lot of pins.

Head pins

The best wire to use is 0,6 mm. Wire thickness will depend on the size of the hole in your bead, but use at least 0,4 mm. The length of

the wire is the length of the pin required plus 10 mm to form the pin. **Tools required:** Side cutters, flat or round-nose pliers, Chain–nose piers.

I Create a hairpin bend on one end of your wire with flat or round-nose pliers; the part that folds over need not be longer than about 5 mm.

2 Slowly pinch the two wires flat against each other as close as possible along the length of the fold, with either your Chain-nose pliers or the very back jaw of your round-nose pliers. (Some brands may not have this flat, very strong area at the back which I find most useful.

3 With sharp side cutters, cut the short end of wire as close to the bend in the two wires as possible. The bend must still be there; this is what will prevent your beads from slipping off.

4 Gently squash the pin into a neat shape. Some beaders prefer to lightly hammer this tip flat for a different effect.

Eye pins

These are useful for making double ended beaded linked loops. The wire thickness will depend on the size of the hole in your bead, but use at least 0,6 mm (22 gauge). The length of the wire is the length of the pin required plus 10 mm to form the pin. **Tools required:** Side cutters, Chain-nose pliers, round-nose pliers.

I Measure just short of 10 mm (9,9 mm) and make a right angle in the wire using the Chain-nose pliers.

2 Grab the end of the bent tail with the tip of your round-nose pliers and in a fluid motion curl or rotate the wire into a loop back towards the bend, as far as your wrist will turn. Release the pliers. Reposition your hand on the pliers to allow you to continue turning to close the loop.

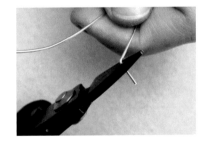

TIP

The position of your pliers and the length of the bent tail in step 1 will determine the size of the loop. This will come with practice. I use the very tip of my pliers to get the smallest possible loops. Find the perfect spot on the jaw of your pliers and mark it for perfect loop sizes every time.

Attaching drop beads (top drilled beads)

A drop bead is a top-drilled bead.

With a wrapped loop

Use a 100 mm length of beading wire, at least 0,4 mm thick. **Tools required:** Side cutters, Chain-nose pliers.

I Grab the wire in the centre with the Chain-nose pliers and pull the two ends towards and across each other to create a triangle shape.

2 Without distorting the shape of the triangle too much, gently thread the bead onto the triangle allowing it to hang freely (it must be able to swing) on the flat base of the triangle, exactly below the wire crossing.

3 With your Chain-nose pliers make an indent in the wire where the tails cross so that this tail stands upright.

4 Hold the upright tail with your Chain-nose pliers and gently begin to wrap the other tail around it, the first coil starting where the

tails cross to secure the triangle formed in step 1. The number of coils depends on your design but make at least two complete wraps.

5 Trim as close as possible to the coil with side cutters. Apply the Sulcas technique (see page 28) if your wire is not tucked in sufficiently.

With flexible beading wire

This is ideal for gemstones with irregularly drilled holes. It is very quick, secure and neat, used for making earrings and drop pendants. Use tigertail and crimp beads. **Tools required:** Side cutters, crimping tool.

I Cut a 20 mm length of flexible beading wire, thread your drop bead onto one end and allow to hang in the centre.

2 Through both tails thread a crimp bead (see simple crimping page 36) and any other beads that you may choose, ending with a crimp again. If you would just like a drop and no additional beads you can use one crimp only.

3 With the crimping tool, take hold of the crimp bead closest to the drop, slide it gently into place towards the drop bead (the drop must just have enough space to hang freely).

4 When you are satisfied that the drop is positioned correctly squash the crimp bead in the simple crimp manner. Try to make sure that the wires are centred to the squashed crimp, so crimp slowly so that you can shift the wires into the middle of the crimp if necessary.

5 Tuck one of the strands of beading wire back through the top, unsquashed crimp bead forming a loop above the crimp. It will now look like a bow.

6 Slowly pull both ends to move the additional beads flush up against the drop and to make the loop above the unsquashed crimp smaller (about 2mm).

7 Squash the top crimp bead into place.

8 Trim the excess wire at both ends of the crimp beads as close to the crimp beads as possible.

With a figure of eight loop

This method is not suitable for heavy beads. Use 100 mm beading wire at least 0,6 mm thick. **Tools required:** Side cutters, Chain-nose pliers, round-nose pliers.

1 Grab the wire in the centre with the Chain-nose pliers and pull

the two ends towards and across each other to create a triangular shape.

2 Without distorting the shape of the triangle too much gently thread the bead onto the triangle allowing it to hang freely (it must be able to swing) on the flat base of the triangle, exactly below the wire crossing.

3 Cut the one wire tail flush with the point where the two tails cross.

4 Cut the remaining tail just short of 10 mm as for a common loop.

5 Grab the end of the 10 mm tail with the tip of the round-nose pliers and curl the wire back towards the flush wire forming and closing a figure of eight.

6 To attach to another object, either thread through the loop or gently twist the loop open as you would for a jump ring and close in the same way.

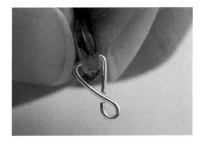

Jump rings

Mostly used for connecting components for such as a chain with the rings on a clasp. Open and close as described here.

Tools required: Two pairs of sturdy pliers. (Chain-nose pliers and crimping tools work well. Round-nose pliers tend to slip and therefore mark the rings.) Jump ring tool (optional but very useful).

1 Grip one side of the jump ring with a jump ring tool/sturdy pliers and the other side with another set of sturdy pliers. The opening of the ring must be in the centre (between the two tools).

2 Using a gentle but firm push-pull action move the one side of the ring away from you and the

other side towards you, enlarging the opening without compromising the shape of the ring.

3 Attach whatever needs to be attached by slipping it into the opening.

4 Close the jump ring using the push-pull action in reverse.

TIP

When closing a jump ring I pull the two ends together and just past each other (1 mm), and then give them one last firm pull aligning them in all directions (almost wiggling the ends exactly into place).

Split rings

Split rings are used when a secure ring is required that will not allow wire or thread to work its way out of the ring. Split rings are much like the kind of ring you would find on a key holder and opens and closes in exactly the same way.

Tools required: Split-ring tool (not essential) or a thin, flat object such as a blade.

1 Wedge the split ring tool or flat object between the two grooves of the ring.

2 Twist the split ring slightly to open it.

3 Feed the required item onto the ring; thread through until it hangs freely in the ring.

Crimping

Two methods are used, namely simple crimping which is actually only squashing the crimp bead, and folded-over crimping. Folded-over crimping is more secure and as the name implies, the crimp is folded over when squashed. The piece that you are making and the materials used will determine which method should be used. Heavy gemstone beads need to be more secure, therefore folded-over crimping is preferable.

Simple crimping

Any base-metal crimps will be suitable, barrel shaped or otherwise. Try not to get very brittle crimps (often very thin) as they crack when squashed. Crimps are used for attaching a clasp, among others. **Tools required:** Crimping tool or pliers for crimping, side cutters.

I Thread flexible beading wire onto a crimp, through the hole for attaching to the clasp and back through the crimp.

2 Use the flat tip at the very end of your crimping tool or ordinary pliers and squash the crimp bead with two gentle but firm presses (crimp, then inspect the first attempt and then crimp again). The crimp should be flat all over with no unflattened parts.

3 Cut the unwanted wire as close to the crimp as possible to avoid a tail that may scratch the wearer.

Folded-over crimping (correct crimping)

Use tube crimps (normally made in sterling silver or gold-filled).
Tools required: Crimping tool, side cutters.

I In the jaw of the crimping tool there are two definite indentations. Holding the tool horizontally, first squash the crimp once firmly in the indentation closest to the hinge (w-shaped). You will

note that the crimp bead has been dented.

2 Move the tool to a vertical position and, using the front indentation with the back of the dented crimp pointing towards the hinges, squash the crimp again, thereby folding it in half.

3 Now use the flat tip of the tool at the very end and give the crimp one more firm squash to be sure that everything is perfectly secure.

4 Trim excess wire with the shallow side of the side cutters.

TIP

I often leave a small 5 mm tail when cutting if my beads are going all the way up to the top of the clasp. Then the excess wire can lie flat in the bead instead of having a small tail protruding from the crimp that could scratch the wearer.

Crimp covers

These are smooth, round, seamed beads open on one side, used for closing over crimps for a professional finish. They are normally used with folded-over crimping, for example a 2 mm tube crimp folded over will fit into a 3 mm crimp cover. **Tools required:** Crimping tool.

I Hold the crimp cover in the indentation closest to the tip of your crimping tool, with the open side facing the open side of the jaws of the tool.

2 Insert the squashed crimp bead that needs to be covered in the crimp cover in the crimping tool.

3 Now very gently apply pressure to the crimping tool, forcing the two open sides of the crimp cover together.

Finishing with French wire

French wire is a thin wire coil in various thicknesses and finishes used to cover and prevent friction on exposed stringing materials, like flexible beading wire and thread. A good all-round size is the medium weight. The cutting is very important. A small pair of nail scissors works very well, so buy them specially for this purpose and store them with your French wire so that they are not used for anything else. **Tools required:** Small pair of nail scissors.

I Measure and cut a 10 mm piece of French wire, ensuring that the coils will not block the passageway for threading.

TIP

Get into the habit of putting away your French wire as soon as you have cut the length you need. This will keep it from tarnishing and avoid it kinking if something heavy is placed on it by accident.

2 String a crimp and thread the 10 mm length of French wire onto your stringing material (in this case flexible beading wire).

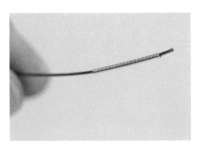

3 Add a clasp, for example, and thread the wire back through the crimp.

4 You will notice that the wire automatically finds its place as you pull it tighter; do not over-tighten as the wire will then bunch up and look very untidy.

5 Squash the crimp bead in place using your preferred method of crimping.

6 Trim the thread and wire as close to the crimp as possible to ensure that it will not scratch the wearer.

TIP

You can vary the size of the loop by cutting a longer piece of French wire for a bigger loop, or a shorter piece for a smaller loop.

Attaching earring components

Most earring hooks, ball and post (studs) and lever backs, have the same basic attachment mecha-nism, namely a ring that can be opened. This is attached as described here: **Tools required:** Two sturdy pairs of pliers.

1 On your earring hook or stud, locate the open end of the ring (the end that is not fixed to the component). Open as you would open a jump ring (either towards you or away from you), just enough to slip in the beaded section.

2 Attach the beads to the ear-ring component.

3 Close neatly flush against the other end of the ring in the same way as opening.

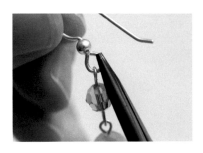

Colour

When choosing beads I find it helpful to make a rough selection and pile the beads all together on a light neutral-coloured work surface, preferably a beading mat that will let the beads stay close together. I then add and take out colours, experimenting with different combinations until I have one that I find most suitable to the look that I want to create. Don't be too conservative; sometimes adding a hint of unexpected colour to a monochromatic colour scheme will make a piece come alive (for example shades of orange with a hint of fuchsia pink).

COLOUR COMBINATIONS

When you combine colours, remain within either a warm range (yellow, orange, red) or a cool range (green, blue, violet), or stick to neutrals (white, cream, beige grey, black and brown).

The best way to choose colour combinations is by using a colour wheel. You would not necessarily always use bright colours so try to imagine these colours in paler versions if using softer colours.

The primary colours are blue, yellow and red. The secondary colours are orange, violet and green (all mixed from the primaries). When the first six colours are further mixed, one primary with one adjacent secondary, they result in a third tier namely yellow-green, blue-green, blue-violet, red-violet, red-orange and yellow-orange.

COMPLEMENTARY COLOURS

Colours directly opposite one another on the colour wheel are called complementary colours. Any colour can be used as an accent with its complementary colour. A primary will always be opposite a secondary colour (for example red and green). Tertiary colours are always opposite one another.

SPLIT COMPLEMENTARY COLOURS

These are formed by a colour and the colours on either side of its complementary colour.

Split compimentary colours make great combinations. I choose a bead I would like to use, then I try to match it to the colours on either side of its complementary and use all thee colours.

TRIADS

Three-colour combinations are called triads, formed by a combination of every fourth colour on the colour wheel. There are three triads on the colour wheel. They can all be combined successfully in beaded pieces.

projects

Simple lariat

Materials and tools

200 cm cord 1 mm thick
16 x 8 mm oval facetted
 gemstones
16 x 8 mm round crystals
24 x 5 mm spring spacers
8 x 8 mm bead caps
1 x tube fast-drying glue
Sharp scissors

Approximate length 145 cm

Knotting the lariat: front view

back view

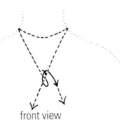

front view

front view

The lariat is a perfect beginner's project – there are no daunting tools required and you can use any beads in any combination. It also allows more advanced beaders a trip down memory lane using high quality beads and cord. This lariat has been strung on beige silk cord, the type that comes with a needle attached. This is very helpful when stringing. The various beads used are Austrian crystals (Star shine), facetted quartz crystal gemstones and oxidised sterling silver caps and daisy spacers.

1 Using a common knot throughout (see page 24) knot one end of the cord 10 mm away from the end and string the following beads in order:
 1 x 5 mm spring spacer
 1 x 8 mm round crystal
 1 x 8 mm oval gemstone
 1 bead cap, large side facing gemstone
Knot as close as you can to the bead cap, measure 40 mm of cord and make another knot.

2 Now thread the following beads:
 1 spring spacer
 1 x 8 mm round crystal
 1 x 5 mm spring spacer

Knot as close as you can to the last spacer, measure 40 mm of cord and make another knot.

3 Thread one oval gemstone and knot as close as you can to the bead, measure 40 mm of cord and make another knot.

4 Repeat steps 1 to 3 another seven times (eight sets in total) starting with the threading of the beads.

5 Add a drop of glue to the very last knots at each end of the lariat. Allow the glue to dry completely (see manufacturer's guidelines for exact drying times) and cut as close to the tip as possible with sharp scissors.

TIP

When selecting beads to thread onto cord be sure that the holes in the beads are large enough for the cord that you will be using. Often after threading the beads a few times the tip of your cord can achieve feather duster status. To avoid this, before starting I glue a 50 mm section at the end of the cord with fast-drying glue, allow to dry completely and cut a long diagonal point across the glued end with sharp scissors. This creates a firm point onto which you can thread the beads.

TIP

Try to get the knots as close up against the sets of beads as possible by making a loose knot as close as you can and slowly pushing it up to tighten with your thumb nail, while holding the thread securely in your less dominant hand.

Variation

Any beads can be used for a lariat; they can all be different to create a very informal and fun look or you can select similar beads and arrange them in a more formal pattern as I have done in this example.

Four-cluster lariat

Materials and tools

2 lengths of 1 mm thick cord
    each 110 cm long
4 x 10 mm round
    facetted beads
4 x 10 mm silver
    spacer beads
4 x 16 mm oval
    gemstone beads
1 tube of fast-drying glue
Sharp scissors

Approximate length 95 cm

Knotting the lariat - back view

Knotting the lariat - front view

1 Holding the two lengths of cord together find the centre point. From the centre point measure 380 mm and knot the two cords together using a common knot (see page 24). Repeat on the other side, make sure that the cords are exactly the same length between the two sets of knots. You will now have two lengths of cord knotted at either end. The space between the knots is 760 mm.

2 The cords that remain loose below the knots will now be knotted individually and threaded individually. Side one strand one, make a knot at 20 mm, add a bead cap (small side against the knot), a large oval bead, a spacer and a 10 mm round bead. Knot the remaining cord as close to the last bead as possible.

3 Side one strand two, make a knot at 40 mm, add a 10 mm round bead, spacer, large oval bead and lastly a bead cap (large side against the oval bead). Knot the remaining cord as close to the bead cap as possible.

4 Side two strand one, make a knot at 25 mm, add a bead cap (small side against the knot), a large oval bead, a spacer and a 10 mm round bead. Knot the remaining cord as close to the last bead as possible.

5 Side two strand two, make a knot at 60 mm, add a 10 mm round bead, spacer, large oval bead and lastly a bead cap (large side against the oval bead). Knot the remaining cord as close to the bead cap as possible.

6 Add a drop of fast-drying glue to each end, knot, allow to dry (see manufacturer's guidelines for exact drying times) and cut as close to the tip as possible with sharp scissors.

TIP

Before final gluing and cutting of the ends, try the lariat on to make sure that the position is correct.

Chunky beads and cord

Materials and tools

8 large (30 mm) oval facetted
acrylic beads (colour 1)
10 x 12 mm acrylic bicone
beads (colour 2)
10 x 12 mm round facetted
acrylic beads (colour 1)
8 x 12 mm glass pearls
(colour 2)
2 x 2 m lengths of 1 mm
beading cord (colour 2)
Sharp scissors
Fast-drying glue

Approximate length 122 cm

Chunky beads are great fun. Acrylic and wooden beads are best because they are not too heavy and for their size are more affordable. If you use flatter beads this necklace could easily be used as a decorative belt for your favourite pair of jeans. Use common knots throughout, see page 24.

1 Knot together the two lengths of cord 12 cm away from the end, leaving the opposite two long ends to thread the beads onto after step 2.

2 Thread a bicone bead and a round bead onto each short end and knot at the end of each cord to prevent the beads from slipping off.

3 Thread one large oval bead onto both long lenths of cord, moving all the way down to the knot made in step 1. Knot together both strands immediately after the bead to secure into place.

4 Thread a glass pearl onto only one strand, move all the way down to the large bead, measure 4 cm from the knot and knot both

strands together, repeat with a round bead, repeat with a bicone.

5 Repeat step 3, then step 4 in the reverse order, namely bicone, round bead, glass pearl.

6 Repeat step 3, then repeat step 4, step 3 and step 5. Repeat the pattern step 4, step 3 and step 5 twice more.

7 Repeat step 2 to end off the remaining ends. They will be approximately 10 mm shorter.

8 Cut any unwanted strands of cord beyond the knots and add a drop of fast-drying glue (see manufacturer's guidelines for exact drying times). Finish off by knotting together the two ends of the necklace.

Multi-strand bracelet with spacers

Materials and tools

84 x 6 mm Czech fire-
  polished round beads
4 multi-strand bar spacers
  (3 or 5 holes)
750 mm beading elastic
  (0,7 mm thickness)
Clear nail varnish
Sharp scissors

Approximate length 18 cm

Variation

Use a different colour bead
for each strand. A combination of brown, beige and
cream glass pearls gives a
very versatile piece.

When choosing beads for this project be sure to use beads that are all the same shape and size. Czech fire-polished beads, glass pearls and crystals are perfect for this. Irregular beads will vary the lengths of your strands which will spoil the effect. I used 6 mm fire-polished beads in iris brown and the spacers are sterling silver with Marcasite detail. Using beading elastic eliminates the need for a clasp, which means this project can be finished in no time. Unfortunately the elastic weakens over time and the bracelet will eventually have to be restrung.

1 Cut three 250 mm lengths of beading elastic.

2 Thread a length with 7 beads and then through one of the outer holes of the multi-strand spacer. Repeat until you have used all the beads and spacers (4x7 beads separated by spacers).

3 Knot the two ends of the beading elastic at the spacer with a square knot (page 24).

4 Repeat steps 2 and 3 for the middle row, then for the last row, taking care to use exactly the same number of beads between the spacers.

5 Apply a drop of clear nail varnish to each knot, allow to dry and trim the ends for a neat finish.

TIP
Do not pull the elastic so that it stretches. It should be knotted un-stretched to avoid making the bracelet too tight. This is particularly important when doing multi-strand bracelets as the tension needs to be the same for each strand.

Easy single-strand bracelet

Materials and tools

30 x 8 mm round crystals or
  glass beads
25 cm beading elastic (0,7
  mm thickness)
1 x 3 mm crimp cover or
  silver ball (large hole)
Fast-drying glue
Scissors
Crimping tool

Approximate length 18 cm

There is elegance in simplicity, as these two easy bracelets made from 6 mm round Austrian crystals (crystal AB) and 6 mm glass pearls respectively show. The length of a bracelet is affected by the size of the beads you use. A standard measurement for a bracelet is 18 cm unstretched. When you use bigger beads, anything from 8 mm up, allow a little more length. Working with beading elastic saves the time and effort of attaching a clasp, but it does mean that the bracelet will have to be restrung at some point as the elastic eventually perishes.

1 Thread all the crystals or beads onto the beading elastic taking care not to stretch the elastic.

2 Knot the two ends of the beading elastic as close as possible to the beads using a square knot (see basic techniques page 24), again taking care not to stretch the elastic. Trim the ends.

3 Apply a drop of glue and use a crimping tool to close a crimp cover over the knot (see basic techniques on page 38) or if you are using a 3 mm silver ball, stretch either end of the knot with one hand (hold one end on your work surface with your thumb) add a drop of glue to the knot and very quickly slide the bead over the knot. Release your fingers.

Variation

Alternate freshwater pearls and crystals for a more classic look.

Cuff bracelet

Memory-wire is a great starting point for beading. It is a very hard wire that has been heat-treated and, as the name suggests, it retains its coiled shape. I thought it would be fun to use it for a more sophisticated cuff bracelet with crystals and sterling silver. I used 5 mm Czech fire-polished beads in Antique Blue, 6 mm Austrian bicone crystals in Indian Sapphire, and 6 mm round crystals in Starshine.

Materials and tools

Memory-wire (1 spool of about six coils, 60 mm diameter)
128 x 4 mm Czech fire-polished beads
34 x 5 mm spring spacers
32 x 4 mm daisy spacers
32 x 6 mm bicone crystals
34 x 6 mm round crystals
1 silver filigree heart charm
2 memory-wire end-caps
Epoxy glue
Wire cutters

TIP

If you cannot find end-caps, use round-nose pliers to bend the wire neatly at the tip of each end in the same direction as the curve of the coil to stop the beads slipping off (add a small bead as a stopper).

Variation

Any beads can be used , but the larger and heavier the beads, the more the wire will stretch under their weight and the less it will hold its shape.

1 Prepare the epoxy glue. Glue one of the memory-wire ends to the wire coil. Allow the glue to dry completely before continuing.

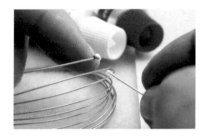

2 Thread the beads onto the memory-wire in the following groupings, moving them to the opposite end of the wire flush against the fitted end cap:

  a. round crystal, spring spacer, bicone crystal, spring spacer, round crystal

  b. 4 fire-polished beads, daisy spacer, bicone crystal, daisy spacer, 4 fire-polished beads

  c. round crystal, spring spacer, heart charm, spring spacer, round crystal

  d. 4 fire-polished beads, daisy spacer, bicone crystal, daisy spacer, 4 fire-polished beads

  e. round crystal, spring spacer, bicone crystal, spring spacer, round crystal.

3 Alternate steps 2d and e 14 times, ending with e.

4 Trim the memory-wire, allowing just enough space for the other end-cap and glue into position. Allow to dry thoroughly before handling the bracelet.

Floating-pearl necklace

Materials and tools

100 cm clear beading nylon,
   3,5 mm thick
21 x 7/8 mm freshwater or
   glass pearls
1 small trigger clasp with
   ring attached
2 small soft crimps
2 x 3 mm crimp covers
1 x 4,5 mm split ring or solid
   ring (if you do not have any
   of these a jump ring can be
   used but be sure to close it
   very carefully as the nylon
   is very fine and can easily
   pass through the space
   where the ends meet)
Fast-drying glue
15 mm cardboard guide (cut
   a 15 mm strip of cardboard
   to measure intervals
   between pearls)
Sharp scissors
Crimping tool (or smooth
   chain-nose pliers)
Masking tape
Permanent marker

Approximate length 45 cm

For this single-strand floating pearl necklace I used glue to position the pearls instead of crimp beads. This is a great time saver although it may make the purists cringe. I have managed to glue crystals successfully but not without wasting a few. The glue tends to make the crystals and glass beads cloudy when too much is applied. I therefore do not recommend this method for glass beads. I used freshwater pearls, alternating cream and warm grey. When applying the glue, use a hard plastic work surface which can be wiped clean rather than working on a table which can be damaged.

1 Tape one end of the beading nylon to the left side of your work surface with masking tape. (Reverse if you are left handed.)

2 Make a tiny mark with a permanent marker on the beading nylon 20 cm away from the point where it has been taped to the work surface.

3 Using the 15 mm cardboard guide continue to make 21 tiny marks on the nylon at 15 mm intervals.

4 Thread all the pearls onto the nylon and tape the other end to your work surface.

5 Slide the cardboard guide under the nylon between the taped end and the first dot to lift the beading nylon from the work surface, keeping the pearls to the right of the dot.

6 Very carefully place a tiny drop of glue on the first dot, rest your glue upright and quickly slide a pearl onto the glued spot.

7 Continue to glue all the pearls in this way, taking care that they do not stick to your work surface. Keep a dry cloth handy to wipe up any spills immediately.

8 When all the pearls have been placed leave them to dry completely (see manufacturer's guidelines for exact drying times).

9 Allowing a 15 mm space at both ends of the pearls attach the clasp to one end and a split ring or solid ring to the other end using a crimp (see basic techniques, page 36).

10 Trim the leftover beading nylon and cover the crimps with crimp covers (see basic techniques, page 38).

TIP

On completion, do not ignore the 15 mm spacing requirement on either side of the clasp. If the last two pearls and the clasp are too close together this may become the heaviest point of your necklace causing it to keep swinging to the front.

Variation

Alternate pearl sizes and/or colours for a different look.

Double-strand floating necklace

Materials and tools

12 x 7/8 mm top-drilled
  pearls (colour 1)
11 x 7/8 mm top-drilled
  pearls (colour 2)
24 x 11° seed beads
  (colour 3)
2 x 55 cm flexible beading
  wire (one strand each
  in colour 1 and 2)
2 x gold crimps
8 mm gold pop clasp
Crimping tool
Side cutters

Approximate length 45 cm

To add interest I used two different colours of flexible beading wire, namely gold and bronze, and alternated top-drilled pearls in natural cream and brown. I threaded the lighter pearls on the darker wire and the darker pearls on the lighter wire. Bronze Japanese seed beads keep the wires together. Alternating the beads on the two wires creates an interesting twist in the seed bead.

1 Holding the two flexible beading wires together thread a clasp and a crimp onto both wires at one end.

2 Use the crimping tool or pliers and squash the crimp into place to secure the clasp (see basic techniques, page 36).

3 Trim the excess wires as close to the crimp as possible.

4 String a seed bead on both stands after the crimp.

5 Add a pearl in colour 1 to one of the strands (preferably a contrasting colour strand).

6 String a seed bead on both strands, push up towards the pearl, leaving about 1 cm.

7 Add a pearl in colour 2 to the other strand.

8 Repeat steps 4 to 7 until all the beads have been used or until the neckpiece is 41 cm long (excluding the clasp).

9 Attach the other part of the clasp to both strands using the crimp as in steps 1 to 3.

✳ Variation

This design makes a lovely bridal necklace and has a delicate floating effect if made up with clear beading nylon (preferably 0,3 mm thickness) using clear crystals and small freshwater pearls (natural cream).

TIP
This design looks great with most beads. The trick is to make sure that the hole of the bead threaded onto the two strands is small enough to just pinch the strands together and lightly hold it all in place.

Slider Bracelet with crystals and pearls

Materials and tools

2 x 400 mm lengths of
   flexible beading wire
4 x 20 mm multi-strand
   spacers (two or three
   holes)
5 small two-hole flower
   sliders – (colour 2)
18 x 6 mm bicone crystals
   (colour 1)
16 x 6 mm bicone crystals
   (colour 2)
2 crimps
12 mm toggle clasp
16 x 5 mm fresh water
   pearls (colour 3)
16 x 11° silver seed beads
Crimping tool
Side cutters

Approximate length 18 cm

TIP

If you need to make the bracelet
smaller by removing beads always
make sure that the end tapers to a
narrow finish before attaching the
bar end of the toggle clasp, otherwise you will not be able to pass the
bar through the ring to fasten the
bracelet.

The beads used for this project need to be very regular in shape to
maintain the uniformity of the pattern. I used 6 mm Austrian crystals in
Chrysolite and light Azure. The freshwater pearls are a very soft peach
pink. The flower sliders are set with crystals in Chrysolite, and seed
beads are clear silver lined. All findings are sterling silver except for the
multi-strand sliders, which are base metal.

1 Attach the two lengths of beading wire to the ring end of the
toggle clasp using a crimp (see
basic techniques, page 36).

2 Thread both beading wires
through a 6 mm bicone in colour 1.

3 Separate the wires and thread
one through the two holes in
the flower slider.

4 String onto each separate
strand a seed bead, a 6 mm
bicone crystal in colour 1, a pearl
and a bicone crystal in colour 2.

5 Thread the separate strands
through the outer holes of a
multi-strand spacer, then add a
6 mm bicone crystal in colour 2, a
pearl, a bicone crystal in colour 1
and a seed bead to each strand.

6 Repeat steps 3 to 5 three
times, then add another
flower slider.

7 Thread both strands through a
6 mm bicone crystal in colour
1, through a crimp bead and the
bar end of the clasp.

8 Loop both wires back through
the crimp and through the
slider. Clamp the crimp in place
making sure there is enough space
for the toggle to move freely.

9 Trim the wire as close to the
slider as possible.

Variation

Sliders are available in many
colours and styles. This can be
an expensive item; therefore
I prefer to use several colours
so that the bracelet will be
versatile for the wearer.

Multi-strand floating necklace

Materials and tools

27 x 7/8 mm freshwater
   pearls
60 silver crimp beads
   (small and soft)
10 mm x 5 mm trigger clasp
1 350 mm flexible
   beading wire
20 mm cardboard guide
crimping tool
side cutters

Approximate length of
shortest strand 45 cm

Although I used flexible beading wire, this necklace also looks beautiful on clear beading nylon (0,35 mm is a good thickness to use), especially as a bridal option. You can also experiment with alternating crystals and different sized pearls. For a more affordable combination simple glass beads of different shapes look very attractive. Be sure not to choose them too big as this will be heavy and weigh the strands down too much.

1 Cut the wire into two lengths of 400 mm and one of 550 mm.

2 String a crimp bead onto the longest strand and squash it in position 155 mm from the end.

3 String a pearl flush up against the crimp, then another crimp bead and squash the crimp bead flush up against the pearl (see basic techniques page 36).

4 Using your cardboard guide to measure the intervals between the pearls, add another crimp, squash into place (20 mm away from the previous one).

5 Add another pearl and a crimp and squash the crimp in place.

6 Repeat steps 5 and 6 for a total of ten crimped pearls on the wire. The approximate measurement should be 240 mm leaving a tail of 155 mm.

7 Repeat steps 2 to 6 using one of the shorter strands but squash the first crimp 105 mm from the end and use a total of 9 crimped pearls for an approximate length of 120 mm, leaving a tail of 95 mm.

8 Repeat steps 2 to 6 using the other shorter strand but squash the first crimp 105 mm from the end and use a total of 8 crimped pearls for an approximate length of 190 mm, leaving a tail of 105 mm.

9 Place the three strands flat on a beading mat; arrange the longest at the bottom, the nine-pearl strand in the middle and the eight-pearl strand at the top.

10 Thread a crimp bead through all three strands at one end leaving a 30 mm space between the first pearl of the top strand and the crimp bead holding all three strands. Squash the crimp bead to secure all three strands, ensuring that the strands do not twist and are crimped in the same order as they lie.

11 Repeat at the other end. I prefer to use a display bust or a person to make final adjustments before squashing the crimp bead and securing the strands at the opposite end.

12 Cut the two shorter strands as close to the crimp bead as possible on both sides leaving only the main strand.

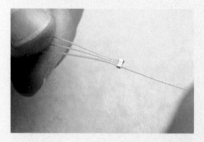

13 From the crimp holding the three strands together, measure 80 mm along the now single thread. Add a crimp and a clasp and crimp into place (see basic techniques page 36).

14 Measure 80 mm at the other end, add a crimp, make a small to medium loop with the wire by threading it back through the crimp and crimp into place.

15 Trim the wire flush up against the crimps on both sides.

TIP

When arranging your beaded strands, before securing them with a crimp, make sure that the strands are equidistant in the middle section, ensuring that the beads are off-centre from each other and are not aligned one on top of another.

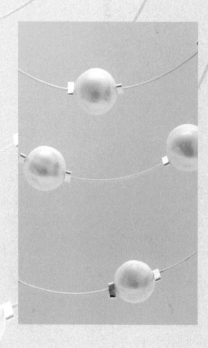

Chain and feathers

Materials and tools

88 cm chain with 4 mm links
25 mm chain with 3 mm links
Large oval, disc-shaped
  metallised plastic bead
  (silver)
9 jump rings
20 mm perfect ring
1 eye pin
2 head pins
Large natural shell pendant,
  round or oval
Large twisted foil bead
  (white)
Medium metallised plastic
  bicone (silver)
Large metallised plastic
  heart pendant
Large acrylic heart bead
  (cream)
Large foil heart bead (white)
20 cm x 1 mm cord (white)
Fast-drying glue
Sharp scissors
1 thong crimp
1 feather (white)
Chain nose pliers
Side cutters
Round nose pliers

Approximate length 88 cm

For this piece, commissioned by a teenage customer, I used a combination of cream, white, silver and natural shell colours. Try to find beads that are not too heavy as this will put too much strain on both the chain and the wearer. I used the metallised plastic beads for this reason.

1 Thread the oval disk-shaped plastic bead onto the eye pin and make a common loop at the end (see basics techniques page 26) then attach a jump ring to both ends (see basic techniques page 35).

2 Link the two ends of the long chain into a jump ring on one end of this bead.

3 Thread the white foil heart onto a head pin and make a common loop and attach a jump ring.

4 Thread the cream acrylic heart onto the remaining head pin, make a common loop and attach a jump ring.

5 Fold the white cord in half, thread the loop through the hole in the shell pendant, take the loop over the loose ends of the cord and pull tight to secure. Now tie the pendant to a jump ring using the loose ends of the cord and a square knot.

6 Thread the twisted foil bead onto one of the cord ends, measure 50 mm from the knot securing the jump ring and knot to secure the twisted foil bead.

7 Thread the plastic bicone onto the remaining cord end, measure 45 mm from the knot securing the jump ring and knot to secure the bicone. Add a drop of glue to both knots, allow to dry (read the manufacturer's instructions) and trim using sharp scissors.

11 Attach the white foil heart, the chain with the cream acrylic heart and the heart pendant, the feather, the shell pendant and lastly the oval disk with the long chain to the large perfect ring using their jump rings.

8 Clamp the feather with the thong crimp and attach a jump ring to the crimp.

9 Attach the heart pendant to the 25 mm length of chain with a jump ring then attach the other end of the chain to the perfect ring with another jump ring.

10 Attach the acrylic heart to the middle of this chain using its attached jump ring.

*

Variation

Experiment with the
various antique finish
chains and big beads in
jewel colours for a more
rustic look.

Gemstone and crystal necklace

Materials and tools

5 large oval gemstones (about 16 mm)

4 x 10 mm round crystals (colour 1)

6 x 8 mm round crystals (colour 2)

3 x 6 mm round crystals (colour 1)

12 x 6 mm bugle beads (silver)

1 g 11° seed beads (silver)

29 x 6° seed beads (colour 1)

6 cm fine silver chain

2 head pins

1 trigger clasp (medium about 14 mm)

15 x 4 mm flat daisy spacers

8 x 8 mm flat daisy spacers

6 x 5 mm flat spring spacers

4,5 mm split ring (if the clasp does not have a ring attached)

60 cm flexible beading wire (0,35/0,45 mm)

2 cm French wire (optional)

2 crimps

1 pendant attachment

Crimping tool

Side cutters

Round nose pliers

Approximate length 47 cm

I find working with gemstones very rewarding. I combined Mukite (matt) with Austrian crystals in light Amethyst Satin and Golden Shadow. The 6° Japanese seed beads are light topaz AB matt and the 11° silver seed beads and the bugle beads are clear silver lined. Since I used gemstones and crystals, it made sense to interspace them with oxidised sterling silver findings and spacer beads. When choosing beads, look out for multi-coloured stones for your focal beads and simply match your crystals to the different colours that you see in the stones, the contrast of the matt finish with the crystals is particularly striking. Necklaces with pendants made with an extension chain fitted to the clasp allow the wearer to adjust the pendant position in relation to the outfit with which it is being worn.

1 Sort your gemstones into similar pairs by colour and shape. Select the most attractive one for the centre drop (focal bead).

2 On a head pin thread a 4 mm daisy spacer, the focal bead and another daisy spacer, ending with a wrapped loop linking it onto the pendant spacer (see basic techniques page 28).

3 Thread the pendant attachment with the attached drop onto the beading wire, take it to the middle of the wire and add the beads onto both sides as follows:

a. 6° seed bead

b. 4 mm daisy spacer

c. 10 mm round crystal (colour 1)

d. 8 mm daisy spacer

e. oval gemstone

f. 8 mm daisy spacer

g. 8 mm round crystal (colour 2)

h. 6° seed bead

i. 5 mm spring spacer

j. 10 mm round crystal (colour 1)

k. 5 mm spring spacer

l. 6° seed bead

m. 8 mm round crystal (colour 2)

n. 8 mm daisy spacer

o. oval gemstone

p. 8 mm mm daisy spacer

q. 8 mm round crystal (colour 2)

r. 5 mm spring spacer

s. 6 mm round crystal (colour 1)

4 For the next 11 cm on both sides of the necklace use 4 mm daisy spacers, seed beads and bugle beads, repeating the following pattern (total length 45 cm excluding extension chain and clasp):

a. 4 mm daisy spacer

b. 11° seed bead

c. 6° seed bead

d. 11° seed bead

e. 6 mm bugle bead

f. 11° seed bead

g. 6° seed bead

h. 11° seed bead

5 End on a 6° seed bead. Add a crimp and another 6° seed bead, finishing with French wire (see basic techniques page 39) and the clasp. Crimp into place.

6 At the other end, finish with a seed bead, a crimp, another seed bead, French wire and the extension chain. Crimp into place.

7 On a head pin thread a 6 mm round crystal, a 4 mm daisy spacer, a 6° seed bead and end with a common loop (see basic techniques page 26). Attach to the extension chain.

TIP

Before crimping to attach the toggle always check that your design is correct and that you have not duplicated or missed beads. If you have duplicated a seed bead it is not necessary to restring the entire piece. Simply crack the unwanted bead with your crimping pliers and remove.

Variation

This design looks very striking made up in dramatic onyx gemstones (black) mixed with black diamond (dark grey) and Silver Shade (vintage silver) Austrian crystals for evening wear. Using white alabaster gemstones with white opal (milky white) and moonlight (clear with a twinkle) Austrian crystals will give a softer finish.

Classic pearl necklace

Materials and tools

24 x 8/9 mm freshwater
   pearls (colour 1)
   approximate quantities
   for pearls as sizes vary
   according to quality
   and shape.
24 x 8/9 mm freshwater
   pearls (colour 2)
1 large gemstone
4 x 4 mm silver daisy spacers
2 crimps
2 x 1 cm lengths French wire
   (optional)
2 g 11° or 15° Japanese seed
   beads (clear silver lined)
1 x 15 mm silver toggle clasp
1 x long head pin
60 cm flexible beading wire
Crimping tool (or chain nose
   pliers without teeth)
Side cutters
Round nose pliers

TIP

If you intend making an extra long length of pearls, use the best quality flexible beading wire that does not kink if bent. It is well worth the investment and will give the movement expected in a long strand. Flexible beading wire ranges from seven to 49 strands, the latter being the most flexible.

Traditionally pearls are knotted on silk cord. This is a much simpler and quicker way to achieve a similar and longer lasting classic look. The number of pearls required may vary as sizes vary according to quality and shape. Err on the side of caution and buy a few more than specified. I used a lovely moonstone as the focal bead and alternated natural cream and mink pink pearls interspaced with clear silver-lined 11° Japanese seed beads. The findings and daisy spacers are sterling silver.

1 Thread a 4mm daisy spacer, gemstone and another daisy spacer on to a headpin and end with a wrapped loop (see basic techniques page 27).

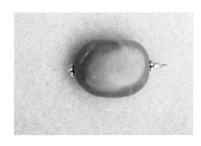

2 Thread a 4 mm daisy spacer onto the flexible beading wire followed by the pendant and another daisy spacer, and move these to the centre of the wire.

3 Start threading the pearls using colour 1 on either side of the pendant, followed by a seed bead, a colour 2 pearl, a seed bead and a colour 1 pearl.

Approximate length 48 cm
without pedant

4 Repeat until all the pearls have been used up and a total length of 47 cm is reached.

5 Finish off by attaching the two parts of the toggle clasp to the two ends, using crimps (see basic techniques page 36).

6 If the flexible beading wire does not fit back through the last pearl you can use a bead reamer (see page 19) to enlarge the hole. Otherwise use a seed bead on either side of the crimp to hold the wire to ensure that it does not scratch the wearer.

Variation

A classic pearl necklace can be made in the same way without a drop. For the piece photographed with the two-coloured necklace I used 7/8 mm fresh-water pearls in natural cream with clear silver-lined II° Japanese seed beads.

Garnet necklace with drop

Materials and tools

65 cm flexible
  beading wire
6 cm link chain (4 mm)
2 head pins
2 x 1 cm French wire
  (optional)
2 crimps
2 x 4 mm bicone crystals
  (colour 3)
2 x 4 mm bicone crystals
  (colour 1, same colour
  as garnet)
37 x 6 mm disc-shaped
  round garnets
33 x 4 mm bicone crystals
  (colour 2)
67 x 4 mm silver
  daisy spacers
60 cm x 0,4 mm
  beading wire
Crimping tool
Side cutters
Round-nose pliers

Approximate length 45 cm
without drop

I used disc-shaped facetted garnets with Austrian bicone crystals in Crystal Copper and Crystal Brandy for a rich, warm effect. This design will work equally well with any other flattish gemstone with a regular shape. Choose crystals that will complement the gemstone colour.

1 Start by making the drop. Thread a disc-shaped garnet onto a head pin and close with a wrapped loop (see basic techniques page 27).

2 Use the 0,4 mm beading wire and connecting wrapped loops (see page 28) to link this to another garnet, followed by two more garnets and a 6 mm crystal. This is the drop.

3 Loop the drop onto the flexible beading wire and take it to the centre.

4 String the following beads in the order given on either side of the drop:

a. 4 mm crystal (colour 2)

b. 4 mm daisy spacer

c. garnet

d. 4 mm daisy spacer, 4 mm crystal (colour 2), 4 mm daisy spacer, garnet

e. 4 mm daisy spacer, 6 mm crystal, 4 mm daisy spacer, garnet

f. 4 mm daisy spacer, 4 mm crystal (colour 2), 4 mm daisy spacer, garnet

5 Repeat step 4f 13 times or until each side of the necklace from the drop measures 23 cm. End with a 4 mm daisy spacer, add a crimp and a 4 mm crystal (colour 1).

6 Add French wire if you prefer and crimp one end of the necklace attaching the clasp.

7 Add French wire to the other end and make a loop, attaching the chain, and crimp.

8 On the remaining head pin thread a 4 mm crystal (colour 2) a 4 mm daisy spacer and a garnet and close with a common loop (see page 25), attaching it to the extension chain.

Wrapped loop bracelet

Materials and tools

1 spool 0,4 mm
   silver-plated
   copper wire
6 x 7/8 mm freshwater
   pearls (colour 1)
4 x 6 mm bicone crystals
   (colour 2)
3 x 6 mm bicone crystals
   (colour 3)
10 x 4 mm daisy spacers
2 x 8 mm silver bead caps
Small (9 mm) toggle clasp
Round nose pliers
Side cutters

Approximate length 18 cm

TIP

To lengthen the bracelet slightly add an extra beaded loop to the bar end of the clasp, always making sure that the beads taper and are not too large to pass through the ring when fastening.

Most colour combinations will work with this design. When you combine pearls and crystals, try to select the pearls first as crystals come in many different colours and are easier to match with pearls. I used pearls in a rich bronze colour with Austrian bicone crystals in light peach and light Colorado Topaz Satin. Use good quality sterling silver findings when working with pearls and crystals.

1 Attach a bicone crystal in colour 2 to the ring end of the toggle clasp with a wrapped loop and make another wrapped loop on the other side of the crystal (see basic techniques page 28).

2 To this loop, attach a new wrapped loop, thread on a bead cap (small side first), a pearl and a 4 mm daisy spacer and close with another wrapped loop.

3 Attach the rest of the beads with wrapped loops as follows:
   a. 1 bicone (colour 3)
   b. 1 daisy spacer, 1 pearl and
      1 daisy spacer
   c. 1 bicone (colour 2)

   d. 1 daisy spacer, 1 pearl and

   1 daisy spacer
   e. 1 bicone (colour 3)
   f. 1 daisy spacer, 1 pearl and
      1 daisy spacer
   g. 1 bicone (colour 2)
   h. 1 daisy spacer, 1 pearl and
      1 daisy spacer
   i. 1 bicone (colour 3)

4 Attach the next loop, thread a daisy spacer, a pearl and a bead cap, (large side facing the pearl) and close the loop.

5 Attach the last colour 2 bicone with a wrapped loop, thread the wire on the other side through the bar end of the toggle clasp and close with a wrapped loop.

Simple earrings

Materials and tools

2 x 6 mm round crystals
2 x 7/8 mm freshwater
   pearls
2 x 4,5 mm daisy spacers
2 x 5 mm spring spacers
Earring components
   (studs or hooks)
2 head pins
Round nose pliers
Side cutters

Variation

For a matching bracelet, use
the steps on page 73 but omit
the bead caps and use round
crystals in Golden Shadow
combined with natural cream
coloured pearls.

This is a very basic earring that can be modified in many different ways
by adding or omitting beads and adjusting the length of the headpin accordingly. Use good quality components and work carefully when making the common loop and attaching the earring component to ensure
that there is movement in the earrings.

1 Stack the beads in the following
order on each head pin
   a. 1 daisy spacer
   b. 1 pearl
   c. 1 spring spacer
   d. 1 round crystal

2 Make a common loop on the
other side of each head pint
(see page 24).

3 Link the looped beads onto
the ear wire as described in
basic techniques (see page 39).

TIP
Sometimes the holes in the pearls are
too small for average head pins. If
you cannot thread the headpin
through the holes, either use a bead
reamer to enlarge the hole or make a
head pin (see page 30) using a slightly thinner beading wire.

Gemstone tiles and crystal necklace

Materials and tools

23 square or rectangular
  gemstone tiles
5 x 8 mm round crystals
1 x 4 mm daisy spacer
6 x 6 mm bicone crystals
5 x 12 mm gemstone ovals
  (same gemstone as
  the tiles)
1x 8 mm spacer
6 cm silver chain
  (4 mm links)
5 mouldable bead caps
Medium S-clasp
3 x 4,5 mm split rings
2 head pins
38 eye pins or 1 spool 0,6
  mm silver-plated
  beading wire
Round-nose pliers
Chain-nose pliers
Side cutters

Approximate link 50 cm
excluding drop

Gemstones used in this necklace are very high quality Kianite tiles and ovals. I love the beautiful ice blue colour and the way light reflects through the tiles. I combined them with Austrian crystal rounds and bicones in Indian Sapphire. With stones of this quality it goes without saying that all the findings and spacers should be oxidised sterling silver. This piece was finished with a beautiful Marcasite S-clasp.

1 Use connecting loops (see page 26), link six sets of three gemstone tiles and two sets of five gemstone tiles using eye pins.

2 Thread five 6 mm bicones and four 8mm round crystals onto eye pins one by one and close each one with a common loop.

3 Using an eye pin, thread each of the five oval gemstones with a bead cap encasing it, and close with a loop. Gently mould each bead cap to take the shape of the oval bead it encases.

TIP

Add more beaded links to the back of the necklace to lengthen it if required. Mix the gemstones with freshwater pearls to keep the cost down.

4 For the detail on the extension chain thread together on a head pin a 6 mm bicone, a daisy spacer and a gemstone tile, end with a loop and attach to the extension chain.

5 Make the drop: thread together on a head pin a 6 mm bicone, an 8 mm spacer and an 8 mm round crystal. End with a common loop and attach to the encased en of an oval gemstone prepared in step 3. Attach a split ring to the top of the drop (see page 35).

6 Connect all the prepared beads on looped pins as follows by first attaching two 6 mm bicones to the split ring at the top of the drop attachment. Now split these and attach the rest of the beads to both sides as follows:

a. a three-tile strand
b. an 8 mm round crystal
c. an oval gemstone
d. a 6 mm bicone crystal
e. a three-tile strand
f. an 8 mm round crystal
g. an oval gemstone
h. a 6 mm bicone crystal
i. a five-tile strand

7 Add a split ring and then the S-clasp to one end of the necklace closing this end of the split ring to secure it.

8 Add the last split ring to the extension chain and attach to the other end of the necklace to close it.

Multi-strand gemstone and pearl necklace

Materials and tools

8 x 7/8 mm freshwater pearls
5 x 8 mm oval gemstones
6 x 8 mm bicone crystals
  (colour 1)
3 x 4 mm bicone crystals
  (colour 1)
6 x 8 mm round crystals
  (colour 2)
4 x 8 mm round crystals
  (colour 3)
4 x 4 mm bicone crystals
  (colour 4)
4 x 5 mm bicone crystals
  (colour 4)
9 x 5/8mm twisted cylinder
  beads (colour 4)
1 x doughnut shaped crystal
  (colour 1) or 8 mm round
2 x 3-to-1 connectors
3 x 5 mm spring spacers
3 x 4 mm daisy spacers
4 crimps
28 x 11° seed beads
  (clear silver lined)
26 x 6 mm bugle beads
  (clear silver lined)
6 x 4,5 mm split rings
44 eye pins
1 head pin
6 cm chain (4 mm links)
2 x 20 cm lengths of flexible
  beading wire (tigertail)

2 x 10 mm French wire (optional)
12x6 mm clasp with ring
Chain-nose pliers
Round-nose pliers
Side cutters
Crimping tool

By choosing your colours cleverly, you can combine just about any beads in one piece. For this eye-catching multi-strand necklace I used clear Austrian crystals with Silver Shade, light Azure Satin and Black Diamond AB. They combined well with pearls in a cool grey. The gemstones are grey agate and worked very well with the grey lustre of the twisted cylinder beads in Czech pressed glass.

Link the following beads using eye pins and common loops (see basic techniques page 25):

a. **Strand one:** 1 x 5 mm bicone crystal (colour 4), 1 x gemstone, 1 pearl, 1 x cylinder bead, 1 x 8 mm bicone (colour 1), 1 pearl, 1 x 8 mm bicone (colour 1), 1 x cylinder bead, 1 x pearl, 1 x gemstone, 1 x 5 mm bicone (colour 4).

Attach a split ring to both ends of the strand (see basic techniques page 35).

b. **Strand two:** 1 x 4 mm bicone (colour 1), 1 x cylinder bead, 1 x 8 mm round (colour 3), 1 x gemstone, 1 x 5 mm bicone (colour 4), 1 x pearl, 1 x 8 mm round (colour 2), the dough-nut shaped crystal, 1 x 8 mm round (colour 2), 1 x pearl, 1 x 5 mm bicone crystal (colour 4), 1 x gemstone, 1 x 8 mm round (colour 3), 1 x cylinder bead, 1 x 4 mm bicone (colour 4). Attach a split ring to both ends (see basic techniques page 35).

c. **Strand three:** 1 x cylinder, 1 x 8 mm bicone (colour 1), 1 x pearl, 1 x 8 mm round (colour 2), 1 x cylinder, 1 x gemstone,

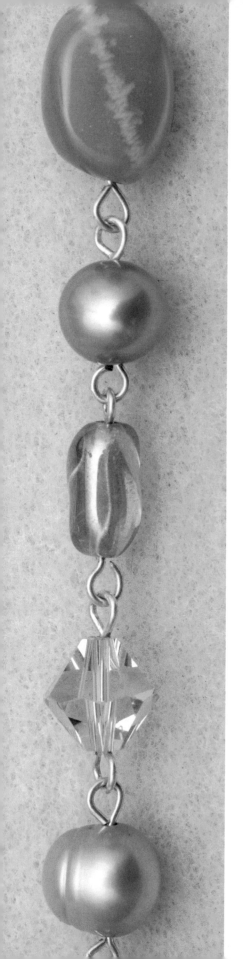

1 x 8 mm round crystal (colour 3), 1 x 4 mm bicone (colour 4) , 1 x pearl, 1 x 4 mm bicone (colour 4), 1 x 8 mm round (colour 3), 1 x gemstone, 1 x cylinder, 1 x 8 mm round (colour 2), 1 x 8 mm bicone (colour 1), 1 x pearl, 1 x cylinder. Attach a split ring to both ends (see basic techniques page 35).

2 Attach the strands to the 3-to-1 connector with the longest strand to the bottom holes, the medium strand to the middle holes and the shortest strand to the top holes.

3 Thread one length of flexible beading wire onto the other side of the 3-to-1 connector, neatly securing the loop with a crimp leaving a small, neat 2 mm loop to allow some room for movement. Repeat on the other side.

4 String the following beads on both strands of beading wire you have just attached:
a. 1 x 8 mm round crystal (col 2)
b. 1 spring spacer
c. 1 x 8 mm bicone (colour 1)

d. 1 x 4 mm daisy spacer
e. 1 x 4 mm bicone (colour 4)
f. 1 bugle bead and 1 x 11° seed bead (repeat 13 times)
g. 1 x crimp and a seed bead

5 Add French wire (optional) and crimp one end of the necklace attaching the clasp. Repeat at the other end attaching the extension chain.

6 On the head pin thread a 4 mm bicone (colour 1) a 4 mm daisy spacer, a 5 mm spring spacer and a twisted cylinder bead. Close with a common loop (see basic techniques page 25) and attach to the end of the extension chain.

Variation

This design can be changed to a double-strand using a 2-to-l connector, or use a double-strand spacer and finish with a multi-strand clasp.

Approximate length of inner strand 45 cm

TIP
If you are doing your own combination, be aware that the beads need to be graded in size. Use the smaller beads close to the 3-to-1 connector to ensure that the strings can sit neatly when attached.

Long necklace with gemstones and crystals

Materials and tools

12 long elliptical gemstones
20 small elliptical gemstones
6 x 6 mm round crystals
   (colour 1)
2 x 6 mm round crystals
   (colour 3)
5 x 8 mm round crystals
   (colour 3)
2 x 8 mm round crystals
   (colour 2)
4 x 8 mm bicone crystals
   (colour 4)
1 spool 0,6 mm beading wire
1 spool 0,4mm beading wire
Round-nose pliers
Side cutters

*Variation

This piece was intended to be inspirational rather than a set pattern. Experiment with whatever you have, group beads in clusters and see if they make a good colour story. Add and remove colours until you are happy with the combination.

This is a fun piece to make, so don't fuss too much about matching the pattern exactly. Just do your own thing and if you are using beautiful gemstones and crystals you cannot go wrong. I used polished Mukite, a gemstone indigenous to Australia, with Austrian crystals in Sun Satin, light Colorado Satin, light Amethyst Satin, light Colorado Topaz AB, and Topaz. If you cannot find all the satin colours, look at your gemstones carefully and simply match the colours you see in them.

The size of the holes drilled in gemsones vary, therefore I keep at least two thicknesses of wire handy when working with gemstones. I always use the thickest wires that will go through the hole.

Using the wrapped loop technique attach all the beads in the following random order:

a. small gemstone
b. 6 mm round crystal (colour 1)
c. large, then small gemstone
d. small gemstone
e. 8 mm round crystal (colour 3)
f. small gemstone

g. 6 mm round crystal (colour 1)
h. large gemstone
i. 8 mm bicone crystal (col 4)
j. small, then large gemstone
k. 8 mm round crystal (colour 3)
l. small gemstone
m. 6 mm round crystal (colour 1)
n. small gemstone
o. 8 mm round crystal (colour 2)
p. large, then small gemstone
q. 8 mm round crystal (colour 3)
r. large gemstone
s. 6 mm round crystal (colour 1)
t. 2 x small gemstones
u. 8 mm round crystal (colour 3)
v. small gemstone
w. 8 mm bicone crystal (col 4)
x. large, then small gemstone
y. 6 mm round crystal (colour 1)
z. small gemstone, large gemstone, small gemstone
aa. 8 mm bicone crystal (col 4)
bb. small, then large gemstone
cc. 6 mm round crystal (col 3)
dd. large, then small gemstone

Approximate length 122 cm

ee. 8 mm round crystal (col 2)
ff. small, then large gemstone
gg. 6 mm round crystal (col 1)
hh. small gemstone
ii. 8 mm round crystal (col 3)
jj. 2 small gemstones, large gemstone
kk. 8 mm bicone crystal (col 4)
ll. 6 mm round crystal (col 3)
mm. small, then large gemstone

2 Join the two ends of the
necklace as you do not need
a clasp for a necklace of this
length.

TIP

Use your crimping tool and apply the
Sulcas technique (see basic techniques page 39) with all the wrapped
loops to ensure neat loops with no
wire sticking out that will scratch the
wearer or catch on clothes.

Gemstone beads and chips with crystals

Materials and tools

4 x large irregular shaped
   gemstone beads
39 medium gemstone chips
60 cm length flexible beading
   wire
2 x crimps
1 magnetic clasp
16 x 6 mm bicone crystals
19 x 4 mm daisy spacers
22 x 11° matt seed beads
   (same colour as the
   crystals)
2 x 10 mm French wire
   (optional)
Crimping tool
Side cutters

Combining beads and chips of the same gemstone gives an interesting effect. I used matt blue lace agate with crystal champagne Austrian crystal bicones. These were beautifully offset by silver-lined Japanese seed beads in a light honey colour with a matt finish. The good quality magnetic clasp I used is very strong, but an ordinary toggle clasp will also work well as a closure option. The approximate length is 50 cm.

1 Begin threading in the following sequence, taking the beads to the middle section of the flexible wire (leaving a tail of the same length on both sides):
   a. 1 crystal
   b. 1 daisy spacer
   c. 1 chip
   d. 1 seed bead
   e. 1 chip
   f. 1 seed bead
   g. 1 chip
   h. 1 daisy spacer
   i. repeat the above sequence twice more (three sets in total) ending with a crystal on both sides

2 Select two large gemstone beads of similar size and shape and string one onto each side.

3 Repeat steps 1a to h on both sides of beading wire.

4 Thread one of the two remaining large gemstones onto each side.

5 Repeat steps 1a to h once on each side. End with a crystal.

6 Add French wire (optional) and finish one end of the necklace attaching the clasp with a crimp (see basic techniques page 36).

7 Repeat at the other end attaching the other side of the clasp.

✴ Variation

This piece looks beautiful if you use clear quartz gemstones (preferably matt as the contrast against the crystals is very striking) and alternate multi-coloured seed beads and crystals.

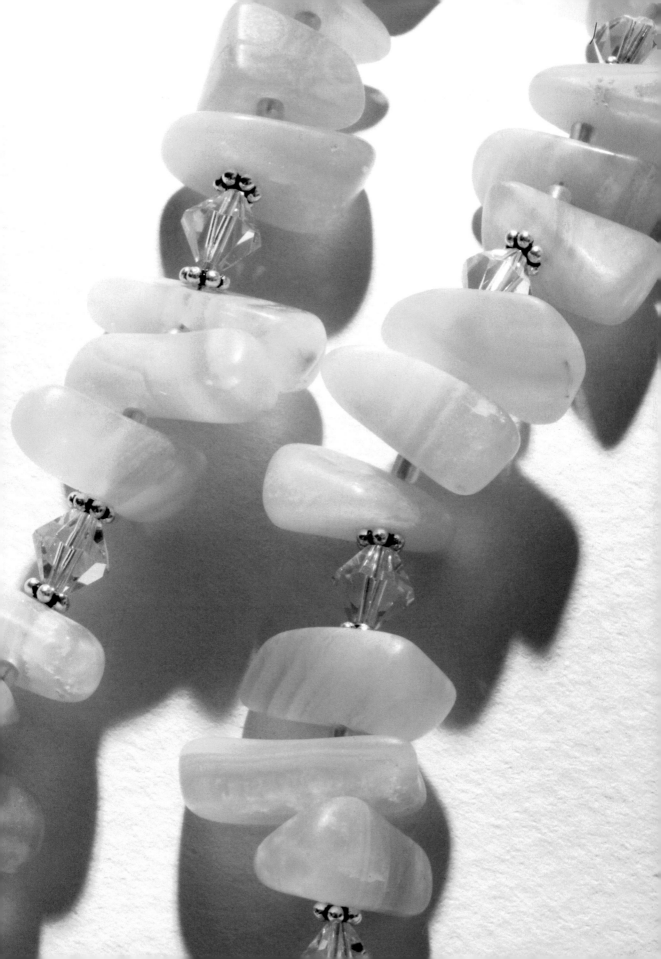

Delicate charm bracelet

Materials and tools

19 cm chain (5 mm link)
4 x 10 mm pressed-glass
   leaves
4 x 8 mm pressed-glass
   bevelled hearts
5 x 10 mm pressed-glass
   shells
4 x 12 mm gemstone hearts
17 head pins
8 mm trigger clasp with ring
Side cutters
Round-nose pliers
Chain-nose pliers

Charm bracelets are a great way of using up odd leftover beads from previous designs. With quality beads I prefer a less full bracelet so that each bead gets to be seen. If you are using fun beads and some ugly ducklings in between, by all means add lots. Thirty or more would be considered a full charm bracelet. Here I used a combination of rose quartz facetted hearts and Czech pressed-glass leaves, shells and hearts. Any delicate chain can be used but I thought this siver chain with its heart-shaped links worked particularly well with the heart theme.

1 Attach the clasp to the chain with the ring.

2 Thread each bead onto a head pin and make a common loop on the other side (see basic techniques, page 25).

3 Lay the chain out and plan the placement of the beads at equal intervals (about three links between beads).

4 Attach the beads by opening the loops, linking them onto the chain and closing the loops.

TIP

For a more chunky charm bracelet, use bigger beads on thicker chain with bigger links. But you may need to attach the beads with jump rings as the standard loops may now be too small to give your charms flexibility and movement on the increased chain size.

Approximate length I8 cm

Variation

For an elegant option use 4/5 mm fresh-water pearls,
with 6 mm round crystals and assorted gemstone hearts.

Handbag tassel

Materials and tools

7 cm length chain (8 mm oval links)

large jump ring (12 mm)

1 bag clip

3 metallised acrylic heart charms (small, medium and large)

2 metal flower charms

3 metal leaves

3 large foil beads, different shapes

2 pearls

Decorative 8 mm metal bead

2 wire-coil beads with two beads in different colours inserted

14 medium jump rings

7 head pins

Side cutters

Round-nose pliers

Chain-nose pliers

This design can also be used as a key chain and can be matched to room interiors. I used a bright silver metal theme with cream pearls and white and soft lime-green foil beads. The idea of mixing glass with acrylic is to achieve a classy look without making the decoration too heavy.

1 Thread every bead that does not already have a loop attached onto a head pin. Make a common loop on the other side and attach an open jump ring.

2 Lay the chain out and position your beads. Place the biggest beads and charms first if you are doing your own design.

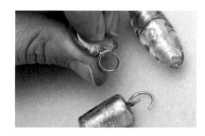

3 Attach the charms and beads in the following order onto individual links of the chain from the top (clasp end)
  a. leaf
  b. wire-coil bead
  c. small heart
  d. pearl
  e. foil bead
  f. decorative 8 mm metal bead
  g. leaf
  h. flower

  i. pearl
  j. foil bead
  k. medium heart
  l. leaf
  m. wire-coil bead
  n. flower
  o. foil bead
  p. large heart

4 Attach the bag clip to the chain using the large jump ring.

Variation

By attaching a weight at the bottom and a badge clip where the clasp is usually fitted these can be used for table-cloth weights.

Vintage crystal necklace

Materials and tools

5 large jump rings (10 mm), linked
15 x 5/7 mm fire-polished teardrop beads (colour 1)
2 x 5 mm fire polished beads (colour 1)
50 cm chain (4 mm oval links)
14 x 4 mm bicone crystals (colour 2)
11 eye pins
1 head pin
10 cm flexible beading wire
2 x 6 mm bicone crystals (colour 1)
1 large top-drilled crystal drop (colour 1)
2 crimps (same colour as chain)
S-clasp (same colour as chain)
Side cutters
Round-nose pliers
Chain-nose pliers
Crimping tool

This charming necklace has an interesting triangle detail before the drop. I used antique nickel chain and findings to create a vintage look with the classic black (jet) fire-polished beads. The colour of the Austrian crystals is an after factory finish called Chilli Pepper. This brings the piece to life. If you cannot find the teardrop beads use a 4 mm with a 5 or 6 mm bead strung one on top of another in its place. This will give you the same effect as a drop. Consider a daisy spacer between the two to add even more detail and movement.

1 Create a beaded link (see basic techniques page 27) by threading a teardrop bead, a 4 mm crystal and then another teardrop shaped bead (narrow sides touching the crystal) onto an eye-pin and close with a common loop. Repeat six times (seven beaded links in total).

2 Make the drop using flexible beading wire (see basic techniques page 31), threading

the beads in the following order: Large crystal drop, crimp, 4 mm bicone, 6 mm bicone, and crimp.

3 Thread a 4 mm crystal, a 4 mm round fire-polished bead and another 4 mm crystal onto an eye-pin and close with a common loop. Repeat.

4 Thread a 4 mm bicone crystal onto an eye pin and close with a common loop.

5 Thread a 6 mm bicone, a 4 mm bicone and a teardrop bead onto the head pin and close with a common loop. (This will be the detail at the end of the extension chain.)

6 Make the extension chain by linking the jump rings and attach the extension detail to one end.

7 Cut the chain into 6 three-link lengths.

8 Link the seven beaded links with three-link sections of chain to create one long strand.

9 Attach the two loops created in step 3 to the ends of the fourth beaded link in the long strand. Cut two five-link lengths of chain and attach one to the end of each hanging beaded link.

10 Now form a triangle by attaching the other end of both chains to the beaded link made in step 4.

11 Attach the drop to the other end of the link.

12 Cut two 9 cm lengths of chain and attach one to each end of the long strand of beaded links.

13 Attach the S-clasp to one end by opening the small end, linking it onto the chain and closing it.

14 Attach the linked jump rings as an extension chain to the oval-linked chain at the other end of the necklace.

Variation

For a beautiful bridal option, use fine sterling silver chain and findings with pearls and crystals.

Approximate length
45 cm without drop

Materials and tools

49 x 7/8mm freshwater pearls
2g 15° or 11° seed beads
22 x 5 mm spring spacers
66 gemstone chips
10 mm bead cone or
    elongated bead cap
6 cm silk cord tassel
1 x 8 mm round crystal
    or pearl
1 x 8 mm bead cap
2 x 4 mm bicone crystals
2 x crimps
80 cm flexible beading wire
Side cutters
Crimping tool

Approximate length 68 cm
excluding tassel

A striking longer-length necklace with a flamboyant tassel drop. Whether you use deep red freshwater pearls combined with garnet chips and a dark red tassel as in the main photograph, or black fresh-water pearls with hematite chips, and Austrian crystals, you will create yourself a traffic-stopper. The piece described here is the second colour option with a total length of 68 cm excluding the tassel.

1 Thread the beading wire through the top of the tassel, pushing the tassel to the centre, and thread 8 seed beads onto both tails on either side of the wire. (The idea is that no wire shows when you place the bead cap or cone over the head of the tassel so you may have to add or remove some beads.)

2 Thread both tails through the 10 mm bead cone with the narrow end at the top.

3 Thread both tails through the 8 mm round crystal or pearl and fit the 8 mm bead cap to the crystal or pearl.

4 Now split the tails and thread a seed bead, a 4 mm bicone crystal and another seed bead onto each tail.

5 Thread the rest of the beads onto both remaining sections of beading wire in this order:

a. 1 spring spacer
b. pearl, seed bead, pearl, seed bead, pearl, seed bead, pearl
c. 1 spring spacer
d. 1 seed bead
e. 6 gemstone chips
f. 1 seed bead

6 Repeat this pattern four more times on both sides.

7 Repeat step 5b one more time on both sides (ream the last pearl).

8 Thread a crimp bead on both ends, thread the ends of the toggle on either side and crimp to secure (see basic techniques page 36).

TIP
When stringing the beads, don't worry too much about them not staying in their correct place as they will be secured into the correct position when you crimp.

Pendant on a thong

Materials and tools

1 x 28 mm glass/crystal
   pendant
1 pinch bail
1 x 2 mm thong crimp with
   loop
1 x 2 mm thong crimp with
   hook
43 cm tubular leather thong
   (2 mm thick)
Scissors
Crimping tool
Chain-nose pliers

Approximate length 44 cm

TIP

When attaching your clasp try to make sure that the clasp is fitted in such a way that if the wearer's dominant hand will be operating the clasp, the pendant will be right side facing out (i.e. if you were to use your right hand to attach the clasp the wrong side of the pendant must be against the wearer's skin and the right side displayed).

A simple crystal pendant on a thong can look truly spectacular. Branded Austrian crystal pendants are all marked. To check for authenticity hold it up to the light and just to the left of the hole you will see the mark (some smaller pendants may not have this mark). I used sterling silver findings with a 28 mm clam shell Austrian crystal pendant in Golden Shadow on a tubular leather thong in metallic gold. The matching earrings were made in no time at all by linking 10 mm cosmic bead crystals to earring components with a common loop using silver head pins.

1 Decide which way you want your pendant to hang if it is not the same on both sides (some Austrian crystals have a coating on one side which looks best facing the wearer so that the light catches the coating through the depth of the glass). Lay it down right side facing up (see tip below).

2 Open the bail, either with pliers taking care not to mark it, or your fingers and close it over the thong and onto the hole of the pendant, taking care not to chip the glass/crystal when closing the bail on the pendant

3 Attach the thong crimps either by folding over the leather or sliding it over the leather and clamping closed (you may have to trim the thong slightly with a diagonal cut to get it to fit.

4 If your thong crimps do not have a fitted hook and eye, attach a split ring to either end and a trigger clasp to one end.

Variation

There are many variations of crystal and glass pendants in every possible colour. Experiment with using multiple strands of hand-painted silk or organza ribbon, use fold over crimp ends, knot your ribbons together before crimping them and add a drop of glue to be sure they are secure.

Elegant crystal cascade necklace

Materials and tools

2 earring chandeliers or
   3-to-1 connectors
6 crimp beads (soft)
3 x 2 mm thong crimps
   with loop
1 x 2 mm thong crimp
   with hook
18 cm tubular leather thong
   (2 mm thick)
3 x 4,5 mm split rings
2g 11° Japanese seed beads
   (clear silver-lined)
6 x 3 mm crimp covers
45 x 4 mm bicone crystals
40 x 6 mm round crystals
21 x 8 mm round crystals
105 cm flexible beading
   wire cut into
   35 cm lengths
Side cutters
Round-nose pliers
Chain-nose pliers
Crimping tool

Approximate length of
inner strand 45 cm

A truly spectacular piece for bridal or evening wear. Make it with Austrian crystals and clear silver-lined Japanese seed beads hanging from a metallic silver leather thong, or use Golden Shadow crystals with a metallic gold tubular leather thong. Findings should be the finest sterling silver or gold depending on your colour choice.

1 String crystals with a seed bead following each crystal except the last in the following order onto one strand of flexible beading wire (this is the top strand):
   a. 4 x 4 mm bicone
   b. 7 x 6 mm round
   c. 6 x 8 mm round
   d. 7 x 6 mm round
   e. 4 x 4 mm bicone

2 String the middle strand as follows, starting and finishing with 2 seed beads and a seed bead following each crystal in between:
   a. 2 seed beads
   b. 7 x 4 mm bicone
   c. 5 x 6 mm round
   d. 7 x 8 mm round
   e. 5 x 6 mm round
   f. 7 x 4 mm bicone
   g. 2 seed beads

3 String the bottom strand as follows with a seed bead following each crystal except the last:
   a. 4 x 4 mm bicone
   b. 8 x 6 mm round
   c. 8 x 8 mm round
   d. 8 x 6 mm round
   e. 4x 4 mm bicone

4 Attach the three strands to the earring chandeliers or 3-to-1 connectors in the correct sequence by using folded crimping (see basic techniques page 36) to secure them.

5 Cover each crimp with a crimp cover (see basic techniques page 38).

6 Attach a split ring to the top ends of the earring chandeliers or 3-to-1 connectors.

7 Halve the leather thong, slide the thong crimps (with loop) over one end of each piece and crimp to attach (trim the thong slightly if necessary to fit the crimps).

8 Link the two thong loops into the split rings attached in step 6.

9 Attach the remaining two thong crimps (one loop, one hook) to the remaining ends of the thong.

10 If you require an extension chain connect the extension chain to the thong crimp with the looped end using a split ring.

TIP

This is a very specific pattern. To achieve the same effect I recommend that you use very high quality beads with the exact shapes and sizes as specified under materials, although different colours can be used.

Wire-wrapped bead bracelet

Materials and tools

8 x 10 mm round facetted
    Czech fire-polished beads
14 x 4 mm round facetted
    Czech fire-polished beads
7 x 4 mm crystal bicones
1 spool 0,4 mm gold-plated
    copper-core beading wire
6 mm magnetic clasp (gold
    plated)
Side cutters
Round-nose pliers

Approximate length 18 cm

TIP

When wrapping the wire coil around the large beads, anchor it first and then move the coil into the desired position with your fingers, instead of trying to get it to be perfect before closing off the wrapping.

In this project the wire is a feature and the head pins are made from the same beading wire as that used for the wrapping. The beads are Czech fire-polished glass beads with a gold lustre and 4 mm Austrian crystal bicones with an after-factory coating called Brandy. For this one, choose your wire first and then find complimentary beads.

1 Make 14 head pins (see basic techniques page 30) and use them to make wrapped loop pendants (see basic techniques page 27) from the 4 mm round fire-polished beads. Once you've closed the wrapped loop, continue wrapping the top of the bead (about four to five additional coils) until the coils cover about a quarter of the bead like a bead cap.

2 Using the 10 mm beads and double the usual length of beading wire create beaded links with wrapped loops (see basic techniques page 27). Do not cut the excess wire but wrap it around the bead as a decorative

feature by coiling it back to the starting point of the beaded link, wrapping it around the bead. One or two coils are sufficient. Use your fingers to hold the new coil in place and to hold its shape.

direction of wire wrapping

3 Anchor the coiled wire around the bead at the base by wrapping over your original starting point wrapped loop about three times. Trim the excess wire and apply the Sulcas technique to the loops (see basic techniques page 29).

4 Use wrapped loops to link the 10 mm wrapped loop beads with the 4 mm bicone crystals, forming a beaded chain (see page 27). Add one of the 4 mm round

fire-polished pendants prepared in step one on both sides of each 10 mm wrapped loop bead as you link the beads to form the chain. (this will create small dangling wire wrapped pendants at intervals in your beaded chain.

5 When you have a chain of six large beaded wrapped loops alternating with 4 mm bicone crystals in a row, link one more 10 mm wrapped bead on both

ends of the strand closing off the ending loops by linking them into one end of your clasp.

Wire-wrapped bead earrings

The matching earrings for the bracelet are really easy to make, especially if you do the wire wrapping of all the beads at the same time as those for the bracelet. You can then assemble the earrings in no time at all.

Materials and tools

2 x 10 mm round facetted
 Czech fire-polished beads
8 x 4 mm round facetted
 Czech fire-polished beads
4 x 4 mm crystal bicones
1 m x 0,4 mm gold plated,
 copper core beading wire
2 earring wires (same
 colour as the wire)
Side cutters
Round-nose pliers
Chain-nose pliers

1 Prepare the beads as for the wire-wrapped bead bracelet (see page 104).

2 Assemble as follows: one 4 mm bicone crystal, one 10 mm round fire-polished bead, one 4 mm bicone crystal, linking one of the 4 mm wrapped fire-polished rounds onto each loop.

3 Attach an earring wire to one end of each of these small chains by opening the loop on the earring wire, slipping on the beaded chain and closing it.

Variations

Double the length of the beaded chain for each pair of earrings to create a long, dangling earring.

Hoop earrings with glass charms

TIP

If necessary, rethread the hoop until you manage to get an equal number of seed beads on either side of the charms. There are many factors that may affect the number of beads needed, namely the varying size of seed beads, thickness of the head pins and wire and also the size of the hoop available, which may vary from supplier to supplier.

These earrings match the bracelet and necklace on page 126. Simple, yet effective, the trick lies in using Japanese seed beads to cover the hoop, as they have a consistently regular hole size, making them easier to thread.

1 Use the head pins and make common loops onto the 4 mm crystal bicones and the twisted ovals.

2 Attach figure of eight loops onto the leaves (see basic techniques page 34).

3 Gently open the earring hoops by pulling the loose side of the ring out of its casing.

4 Thread seed beads onto the hoop until you've covered just more than a third of the hoop

(about 15-16 x 11° Japanese seed beads) then thread the following before threading the rest of the seed beads, covering the hoop:
    a looped crystal
    3 seed beads
    a looped leaf
    3 seed beads
    a looped twisted oval
    3 seed beads
    a looped leaf
    3 seed beads
    a looped crystal

5 Reattach the hoop end into the earring casing and attach the hoop to the earring post using round-nose pliers to open the loop. Thread the hoop and close the loop, crimping slightly to secure.

6 Repeat steps 3 to 5 to make the other earring.

Necklace with lampwork bead and crystals

Materials and tools

1 x 20 mm two-tone or multi-coloured lampwork bead (focal bead)

3 x 5 mm crystal bicones (colour 1)

3 x 6 mm round crystals (colour 2)

1 x 10 mm cosmic shape crystal (colour 2)

1 x 8 mm crystal bicone (colour 1)

8 crimps (colour to match clasp)

1 trigger clasp

800 mm flexible beading wire (match colour to the focal bead)

Side cutters

Round-nose pliers

Crimping tool

Approximate length 54 cm

TIP

Using a flat focal bead gives this necklace a sleek, streamline finish and helps it to sit well.

When I found this beautiful teal, amber and black lampwork bead in a bag of assorted beads I just had to use it as a focal bead. I kept it really simple and used it in this easy piece on black flexible beading wire with Austrian crystals in matching colours, namely Indicolite and Topaz. Antique brass findings completed the picture.

1 Cut the beading wire into 2 strands. Thread the following onto one strand, keeping everything at the end where you are threading:
- a. a crimp
- b. a round crystal (colour 2)
- c. an 8 mm bicone (colour 1)
- d. a round crystal (colour 2)
- e. a crimp

2 Squash the crimps on both sides of the beads (see basic techniques page 36) and trim the short tail as close to the crimp as possible.

3 Repeat steps 1 and 2 on the other strand with the following:
- a. a crimp
- b. a 5 mm bicone
- c. the 10 mm crystal

- d. a 5 mm bicone
- e. a crimp

4 Put the two beaded ends together and thread the following beads onto both strands from the other end:

- a. a crimp
- b. a 6 mm round crystal (colour 2)
- c. the focal bead
- d. a 5 mm bicone (colour 1)
- e. a crimp

5 Measure 60 mm from the top crimp on the first strand and 70 mm from the top crimp on the second strand and squash the bottom crimp threaded in step 4 securing both strands in this position. Squash the top crimp.

6 Separate the strands again, measure 260 mm from the last squashed crimp, thread a crimp onto one strand and attach the clasp by crimping it into position.

7 Measure 260 mm on the other strand and make a loop (about 8 mm) by threading the flexible beading wire back through the crimp and squashing the crimp to secure.

8 Trim the excess wire.

Drop earrings with flexible beading wire

Materials and tools

200 mm flexible beading
  wire (use a shorter piece
  once you have practised
  this a bit)
4 crimps
2 x 10 mm cosmic shape
  crystals
2 ear wires (in the same
  colour as the crimps)
Side cutters
Crimping tool

Making looped drops with flexible beading wire and crimps takes no time at all and all you need then for matching earrings are ear wires. I used the same cosmic shaped crystals as those used for the necklace.

1 Cut the beading wire into two strands of 100 mm and fold one strand in half.

2 Thread the following onto the double strand: a crimp, a crystal and a crimp leaving a 2 mm loop at the top of the fold.

3 Squash the crimps on either side flush up against the crystal with the simple crimping technique (see basic techniques page 36) and cut the excess wire on the opposite end to the loop as close to the crimp as possible.

4 Open the loop on the earwire, slip in the looped crystal and close to attach.

5 Repeat all the steps for the other earring.

Variation

You can add as many beads as you like to this design to make longer earrings. Adjust the length of the flexible beading wire accordingly. I prefer clear beading nylon (0,35 mm) with clear or light coloured crystals or beads so that the wire is not visible through the beads.

Beaded tassel necklace

Materials and tools

Necklace

36 x 7/8 mm freshwater
  pearls (grey)
8 x 15 mm oval facetted
  gemstones (smokey quartz)
6 x 14 mm gemstone nuggets
  (clear quartz)
2 x 12 mm ornate silver
  beads
4 x 8 mm ornate silver beads
1 x 10 mm ornate silver bead
11 x 4 mm crystal bicones
  (silver shade)
1 x 6 mm split ring
1 spool 0,4 mm beading wire
  (silver or plated)

Tassel

1 large gemstone bead
  (Agate)
4 x 5 mm crystal bicones
  (clear)
2 x 15 mm facetted gem-
  stone ovals (smokey
  quartz)
3 x 6/7 mm freshwater
  pearls (grey)
3 x 4 mm daisy spacers
2 x 4 mm crystal bicones
  (silver shade)
1 x 4 mm crystal bicones
  (smokey quartz)

2 clear lentils
1 x 10 mm flat round (clear)
2 x 5 mm drops (clear)
1 drop (clear)
1 x 3 mm silver ball
1 x 4 mm bead (clear)
1 x 4 mm silver bead
1 x 8 mm ornate bead
  (silver & clear)
150 cm x 0,6 mm beading
  wire (silver plated)
3 cm chain
10 head pins or 0,6mm wire
Side cutters
Round-nose pliers

A longer-length necklace with lots of movement from the tasselled gem-stone at the front. I combined grey freshwater pearls, facetted smokey quartz and clear quartz nuggets with ornate silver Bali-style beads and crystal bicones in Silver Shade and used a large facetted agate for the tassel. The wrapped-loop technique is used to link the stones because it is much more secure than the common loop.

1 Start with the necklace. Use the 0,4 mm beading wire and make a wrapped loop (see page 27) on both sides of the following beads or groups of beads linking them as you go along:
  a. 4 x 3-pearl sets
  b. 2 x 4-pearl sets
  c. 1 x 13-pearl set

2 Using wrapped loops as above, connect an oval facet-ted gemstone bead to both ends of the 13-pearl set, followed by a single gemstone nugget at both ends.

3 Attach a wrapped loop to the gemstone nugget and onto the attached wire thread a 4 mm crystal, an 8 mm silver bead and a 4 mm crystal and close the wrapped loop, linking a 3-pearl set made in step 1a. Repeat on the other side.

4 Still using wrapped loops, at-tach a gemstone nugget to both ends, then an oval facetted gemstone bead.

5 Repeat step 3, linking a 4-pearl set made in step 1b. Repeat on the other side.

6 Attach an oval facetted gem-stone bead to both ends, then a gemstone nugget, using wrapped loops.

7 Attach a wrapped loop to a nugget at one end and onto the attached wire thread a 4 mm crystal, an 8 mm silver bead and a 4 mm crystal and close the wrapped loop, linking a 3-pearl set made in step 1a. Repeat on the other side.

8 Attach an oval facetted gemstone bead to both ends, using wrapped loops; connect the ovals with a 6 mm split ring.

9 Attach a wrapped loop to the split ring and on to the attached wire thread the 10 mm silver bead and a 4 mm crystal bicone and close with a wrapped loop.

10 Make the tassel. Use head pins to create the following bead charms ending in a common loop to allow you to move the charms around easily when arranging them:

a. 1 x 5 mm bicone
b. 2 facetted gemstone ovals
c. 1 ornate 6 mm bead
d. 1 x 10 mm flat round
e. 1 pearl
f. 1 pearl, daisy spacer and 5 mm bicone
g. 1 x 4 mm bead, a 4 mm silver bead and a Silver Shade 4 mm bicone
h. 1 silver ball, a silver shade 4 mm bicone, a pearl

11 Use the 0,6 mm wire to create the following bead charms, starting in a drop (see basic techniques page 31 for attaching a drop) and ending in a common loop:

a. 1 drop, a daisy spacer and a 5 mm bicone
b. 1 lentil, a daisy spacer and a 5 mm bicone
c. 1 lentil and the smokey quartz 4 mm bicone

12 Attach all the tassel charms to the 3 cm chain at random taking care to space the charms evenly from top to bottom without having obvious gaps and trying not to have similar beads too close to each other.

13 Use the 0,6 mm wire and attach a wrapped loop to the main necklace at the 4 mm crystal and on to the attached wire thread the large gemstone, end with a wrapped loop linking the tassel chain.

Variation

In the piece photographed on the right I used a combination of beige and natural cream coloured pearls with moonstone ovals, clear quarts nuggets and smokey quartz facetted beads, the shape of which works particularly well for this type of design. The tassel is less detailed as the beads are slightly more chunky.

TIP

If you want to make the necklace longer or shorter, add or leave out pearls in the extended pearl section (step 1 c).

Approximate length 90 cm excluding tassel

Multi-coloured gemstone necklace

Materials and tools

Necklace

7 x 4 mm round gemstone
  beads (colour 1)
7 x 8 mm facetted round
  gemstone beads (colour 2)
6 x 10 mm flat oval gemstone
  beads (colour 3)
7 x 6 mm crystal bicones
  (colour 1)
7 x 6 mm round crystals
  (colour 3)
2 x 5 mm split rings
1 x 6 mm perfect ring (if not
  available use a split ring)
1 heart shaped facetted
  8 mm gemstone (colour 2)
100 mm chain (4 mm links)
  cut into 5 x 20 mm
  sections
15 mm length of chain
  (4 mm links)
1 box clasp
35 eye pins
3 head pins
Side cutters
Round-nose pliers
Chain-nose pliers

I cannot resist a pretty clasp and I designed this necklace, bracelet and earring set around the beautiful amethyst clasp used on the necklace. Gemstones are available in a wide range of colours so I decided to use three colours that work particularly well together, varying the shapes to add interest. The gemstones I selected are carnelian (burnt orange) amethyst (purple) and beryl (green) and I combined them with Austrian crystals in similar colours namely Khaki and Crystal Copper. Silver-plated wire and sterling silver findings finish this piece off. The chain and loops add a clean line to the colourful stones.

1 Use the head pins to create charms that will form the ends of the tassel in the front of the neck-lace, ending in common loops (see basic techniques on page 00):
1 x 8 mm facetted gemstone (colour 2); 1 x 4 mm round gem-stone bead (colour 1); 1 x 6 mm round crystal (colour 3).

2 Use the eye pins to create double-ended linked loops (see basic techniques on page 26) with all the other beads.

3 Make six sets consisting of the following double-ended beaded loops linked together:

a. 1 x 6 mm bicone crystal (colour 1);
b. 1 x 10 mm flat oval gemstone beads (colour 3)
c. 1 x 8 mm facetted gemstone (colour 2)
d. 1 x 6 mm round crystal (col 3)
e. 1 x 4 mm round gemstone bead (colour 1).

4 Attach a split ring to one end of the clasp. Link the bicone side of a beaded set to the split ring, then link a 20 mm length of chain to the opposite end of the beaded set (4 mm round gem-stone side) and then link another beaded set (bicone side first).

Variation

The same technique and very similar design were used in the variation illustrated on the opposite page. I used antique chain and findings combined with with soft pastel-coloured coin pearls, Austrian crystals and gemstones. I just love the soft pastel colours combined with the rugged look of the findings.

Approximate length excluding tassel 48 cm

5 Link a 20 mm length of chain to the other end of the beaded set (4 mm round gemstone side) and then link another beaded set (bicone side first), and link to the 6 mm ring.

6 Repeat step 4 to complete the other side of the necklace.

7 Make the tassel. Attach the 6 mm round crystal charm to the remaining 20 mm chain, link the 8 mm facetted gemstone charm to the remaining double-ended beaded loop, a 6 mm bicone I (colour 1) and attach to centre of this chain.

8 Attach the last 4 mm round gemstone charm to the 15 mm length of chain.

9 Attach both pieces of chain to the pointed end of the gemstone heart by opening the loop, sliding both free ends of the chain onto the loop and closing it again.

10 Attach the tassel to the perfect ring by opening the other loop on the heart, slipping it over the ring and closing to complete the necklace.

Multi-coloured bracelet

Materials and tools

2 x 4 mm gemstone round
  beads (colour 1)
2 x 8 mm gemstone round
  facetted beads (colour 2)
2 x 10 mm flat oval
  gemstone beads
  (colour 3)
3 x 6 mm crystal bicones
  (colour 1)
2 x 6 mm round crystals
  (colour 3)
1 x 5/6 mm split ring
6 x 6 mm perfect rings
1 x 8 mm heart-shaped
  gemstone (colour 2)
30 mm chain (4 mm links)
1 x 20 mm trigger clasp
1 head pin
11 eye pins
Side cutters
Round-nose pliers
Chain-nose pliers

Approximate length 18 cm

I repeated all the gemstones and crystals in the bracelet, but used perfect rings to link them instead of using clusters of beads with chain. For a necklace variation without a tassel, use these instructions and repeat the combination two or three times.

1 Use the eye pins and create double-ended linked loops with all the beads except the heart-shaped gemstone (see basic techniques on page 27).

2 Link them with perfect rings in the following order: 6 mm bicone, ring, 4 mm round gemstone, ring, 6 mm round crystal, ring, 8 mm round gemstone, ring, 10 mm oval gemstone, ring, 6 mm bicone.

3 Attach the clasp to one end and the chain to the other.

4 Thread the heart gemstone onto the head pin (with the head in the point), make a common loop and attach to the end of the chain.

✳ Variation

Choose any of the gemstones or crystals used in the necklace and bracelet for matching earrings. I thought these facetted heart-shaped gemstones would make pretty earrings. The earring posts with gemstone detail were the perfect finishing touch.

Coin-pearl earrings

Materials and tools

2 x 8 mm coin pearls
2 x 6 mm doughnut-shaped
   crystals
2 x 4 mm round freshwater
   pearls
1 pair of earring posts
2 eye pins
4 head pins
Side cutters
Round-nose pliers
Chain-nose pliers

TIP

If you use gemstones for the set (see page 118), try to find earring posts with gemstone detail. If you cannot find these, add an additional beaded link with a 6 mm round crystal in the colour of your gemstone to ensure that the three pieces of the set match.

I used coin pearls and doughnut crystals (Crystal Moonlight) with natural cream freshwater pearls and chain for a set similar to the gemstone and crystal set (see page 118). Choose any of the gemstones or crystals used in the necklace and bracelet for matching earrings.

1 Thread all the pearls onto the head pins and end in a common loop.

2 Use the eyepins and create double-ended linked loops with the crystals, common loops at both ends (see basic techniques on page 27).

3 Link a coin pearl to a doughnut-shaped crystal, then to a round pearl and finally to an earring post. Repeat for the second earring.

Variation

Make a matching bracelet and necklace by following the instructions on pages 122, but using gemstones with pearls.

Charm necklace and bracelet

Materials and tools

14 mm flat diamond-shaped
    foil glass bead
2 x 10 mm round fire-polished
    beads
2 x 12 mm foil glass beads
(flat squares diagonal drilled)
2 x 16 mm twisted oval foil
    glass beads
8 x 10 mm Czech pressed
    glass leaves
4 x 4 mm bicone shaped
    crystals
2 x 8 mm bead caps (shallow)
1 x 4 mm crystal bicone
2 x 7 mm bicone shaped silver
    beads (Bali style)
44 x 6/7 mm glass bicones
23 x 4,5 mm oxidised silver
    daisy spacers
21 x 11° seed beads (match
    colour of glass bicones)
2 x 5 mm split rings (small)
2 x 10 mm French wire
160 mm silver chain
    (5 mm links)
2 tube crimps
7 head pins
0,6 mm wire
50 cm flexible beading wire
Side cutters
Crimping tool
Round-nose pliers
Chain-nose pliers

This project shows you how to make a charm bracelet with an extension that turns it into a necklace. I used a combination of Venetian glass (all the foil beads) in a light sapphire colour, Czech fire-polished beads in crystal with a blue lustre, Czech pressed-glass leaves with a vitrail finish and blue-grey galvanised Japanese seed beads with a matt finish. The chain as well as the metal spacers and beads are sterling silver.

1 Start with the charm bracelet. Use the split rings to attach the toggle clasp to the ends of the chain (see basic techniques page 35).

2 Use four head pins to make common loops onto the tiles and the twisted ovals.

3 On another head pin stack a 6 mm crystal bicone, a bead cap and a 10 mm round fire-polished bead, make a common loop and repeat.

4 Use the last head pin and thread a 4 mm crystal bicone, a daisy spacer and the 14 mm diamond-shaped foil bead. Close with a common loop.

5 Attach figure of eight loops to the leaves (see basic techniques page 34).

6 Lay the chain out on your work surface and plan the placement of the beads at regular intervals (about 3 links between beads). The largest bead must be in the middle (see photograph). Attach the charms by opening the loops, slipping them over the chain in the correct position and closing them again.

7 Make the necklace attachment. String the beads onto the flexible beading wire in this order:
   a. 6 mm crystal bicone
   b. 7 mm silver bicone
   c. 4,5 mm daisy spacer
   d. glass bicone, seed bead, glass bicone
   e. 4,5 mm daisy spacer

8 Repeat steps 7d and e for a length of 310 mm (the number of beads will depend on the size chosen) then repeat steps 7b and a (ending as you started).

9 Add a tube crimp and French wire to each end and attach the toggle clasp and ring by crimping to secure (see basic techniques page 38).

10 Trim the flexible beading wire as close to the beads as possible.

* Variations

Experiment with metallised charms as an alternative to glass beads.

TIP

Do not use beads that are too large as the necklace will become very heavy and sag in the middle when worn as a necklace. If you have chosen slightly heavier beads, use a slightly heavier chain.

Approximate length
bracelet 18 cm; necklace
extension 36 cm

Beaded bracelet watch

Materials and tools

1 g 11° see beads (colour 1)

12 x 6° seed beads (col 3)

24 x 4 mm round Czech fire-polished beads (colour 2)

4 large crystal sliders (colour 4)

2 small crystal sliders (colour 4)

10/12 mm toggle clasp

1 watch face with beading bezel (not bar with pin)

500 mm flexible beading wire

Side cutters

Crimping tool

Approximate completed length 17,5 cm

TIP

Before cutting the wire I prefer to thread the wire all the way back and letting it come out half way through the closest slider, to ensure when I cut the wire after crimping that it does not scratch the wearer as it has a little room to lie flat in the slider.

For the black and silver watch on the main picture I used Czech fire-polished beads in black (Jet) and, instead of a smaller slider, I cross-threaded the two wires through a 4 mm crystal bicone in Black Diamond. When choosing a watch head, make sure that it has a beading bezel (there must be a loop where you can thread your beading wire through on the watch head. Beading watch faces are fairly inexpensive and come in a variety of shapes and finishes including silver, gold, copper, brass, marcasite and rhinestone.

1 Loop one piece of the flexible beading wire through the beading hole at the six o'clock side of the watch, pull through and bring together the ends so that you have two strands of the same length.

2 Thread an 11° seed bead onto each strand followed by a 4 mm Czech fire-polished bead and then a big crystal slider, threading one strand through each hole.

3 Keep working on both strands, threading the beads and sliders as follows:

    d. 4 mm Czech fire-polished bead on each strand

    b. 11° seed bead on each strand

    c. 6° seed bead on each strand

    d. 11° seed bead on each strand

    e. both strands through a small star slider

    f. 11° seed bead on each strand

    g. 6° seed bead on each strand

    h. 11° seed bead on each strand

    i. 4 mm Czech fire-polished bead on each strand

    j. both strands through a big slider

    k. 4 mm Czech fire-polished bead on each strand

    l. 11° seed bead on each strand

    m. 6° seed bead on each strand

    n. 4 mm Czech fire-polished bead on each strand

o. a crimps on each strand

p. 4 mm Czech fire-polished bead on each strand.

7 Repeat steps 1 to 6 on the 12 o' clock side, incorporating the bar side of the toggle clasp.

4 Turn the watch and threaded beads face down and thread the toggle clasp (ring side to six o'clock position) onto each strand of the strap individually. This will ensure that the strap does not twist and is easier to clasp with one hand.

5 Thread each strand back through the beads and the crimps and another one or two beads.

8 Check the strap size on your wrist before you squash the crimps and trim the wire. If you are making it for someone else use the exact wrist measurement plus 10 mm.

9 Squash the crimp beads in such a way that they won't scratch the wearer. Allow a big enough loop for play around the toggle loop. If it is too close up against the clasp it will wear very quickly.

6 Pull both strands simultane-ously to tighten, positioning your fingers exactly as shown in the picture.

10 Cut the wires as close to the beads as you can.

Variation

Use a combination of
fresh water pearls and
Austrian crystals for a very
sophisticated look. You can
also thread beads cross ways
to add width without using
a slider (see cuff bracelet on
page 54).

Drop earrings

Materials and tools

2 x 5 mm crystal drop beads
   (or any top-drilled beads)
200 mm silver-plated
   beading wire (0,4 mm)
2 x 8 mm round crystals
2 x 6 mm crystal bicones
2 x 8 mm bead caps
2 x 5 mm metal
   spring spacers
4 x 4,5 mm metal
   daisy spacers
1 pair silver ear wires
Side cutters
Round-nose pliers

Drop earrings can be as simple or as ornate as you want them to be. The basic technique involves various links and drops, and you can use as may or as few as you like. Here I used black opaque Austrian crystal drops with Bali-style sterling silver spacers and bead caps that have been oxidised to enhance the detail. The oxidised silver findings work particularly well with the black beads.

1 Make a wrapped loop on the drops (basic techniques page 31) taking care that the drops are able to swing freely.

2 On the remaining length of wire, thread the beads in the following order:
   a. daisy spacer
   b. bead cap small side first
   c. 8 mm round crystal
   d. spring spacer
   f. 6 mm bicone crystal
   g. daisy spacer

3 Thread the wire though the loop on the earring wires and close with a wrapped loop. Trim excess wire.

TIP

When using top-drilled gemstones the holes can be very irregular and sometimes very close to the tip. In most cases 0.4 mm wire should be thin enough to pass through the hole of the bead when forming the loop but still strong enough to form the loops without chipping the stones.

* Variation

Just a simple drop without additional beads can look very effective. I use a crimp cover to hide the section where the two wraps meet.

Facetted drop necklace

Materials and tools

1 x 28 mm facetted gem-
stone drop focal bead
(gem 1)
2 x 10 mm facetted gem-
stone drops (gem 1)
4 x 12 mm facetted gem-
stone drops (gem 2)
4 x 4 mm crystal bicones
(colour 1)
6 x 6 mm crystal bicones
(colour 2)
1 string 3 mm round gem-
stones (gem 2)
55 cm flexible beading wire
1 x 9 mm toggle clasp
2 x 10 mm lengths of French
wire (optional)
2 tube crimps
2 crimp covers
Side cutters
Crimping tool

Approximate length 44 cm

These stones are most attractive and do not need much adornment. For this piece I used citrine stones and smokey quartz with matching Austrian crystals: 4 mm bicones in smokey quartz and 6 mm bicones in Jonquil Satin. The small stones are 3 mm polished smokey quarts rounds. Gemstones are often irregular in shape and size and I like to take some time selecting them to be sure that I have the best possible matching pairs for a symmetrical necklace of this nature.

1 On the flexible beading wire string the large focal bead, allowing it to fall in the centre of the wire. Now thread the follow-ing beads on both sides:
   a. 3 mm round gemstones
      (gem 2)
   b. 4 mm crystal bicones
      (colour 1)
   c. 12 mm facetted gemstones
      (gem 1)
   d. 6 mm crystal bicones
      (colour 2)
   e. 3 mm round gemstones
      (gem 2)
   f. 10 mm facetted gemstone
      drops (gem 1)
   g. 4 mm crystal bicones
      (colour 1)
   h. 6 mm crystal bicones
      (colour 2)
   i. 12 mm facetted gemstones
      (gem 2)
   j. 6 mm crystal bicones
      (colour 2)

2 Fill the next 160 mm with 3 mm round gemstones until the total length of beadwork measures 420 mm.

3 Add a crimp and French wire to both ends, then each part of the toggle to one end at a time. Fasten the crimps in place attach-ing the toggle, using folded over crimping (see basic techniques page 36).

4 Cover the crimps with crimp covers (see basic techniques page 38).

Variation

Crystal or glass bead drops can replace the gemstone drops. If you cannot find 3 mm gemstone beads, use 6° Japanese seed beads.

Crochet crystal rainbow necklace

Materials and tools

1 spool of 0,25 mm beading nylon
2 jump rings
432 assorted 4 mm crystal bicones and 8° Japanese drop beads (regular seed beads will also work well in size 6°) Mixed colours
200 mm x 0,6 mm silver-plated beading wire
1 trigger clasp
Size 4 crochet hook
Fast-drying glue
Side cutters
Round-nose pliers
Sharp scissors

Approximate length unstretched 45 cm

A fun project with a striking end result. Don't be put off by the idea that you have to crochet – you only use chain stitch and that is easy enough even if you have never touched a crochet hook. I used 4 mm Austrian crystals in assorted colours mixed with silver-lined Japanese seed bead drops threaded onto clear beading nylon at a ratio of three to one. The beading nylon gives a very twisted and random chain-stitch string, but don't fuss too much about neatness as this is all part of the effect.

1 Without cutting the beading nylon thread all the beads randomly onto the spool.

2 Ignoring the beads that have been threaded onto the beading nylon spool, crochet a 100 mm length of basic chain stitch, then pick up a bead from the spool and slide it towards your work crocheting over it so that it becomes part of the chain. Crochet three

more chain stitches without beads, pick up the next bead. Repeat this sequence, ending with 100 mm chain stitch with no beads, for an unstretched total length of 600 mm (you can straighten it when measuring but do not pull it tight).

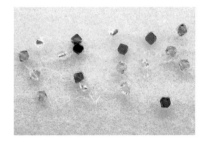

3 Prepare 12 strands (more for a fuller necklace) and knot them together at one end. Knot the strands together at the other end, making sure that there are no obvious gaps where some strands hang much lower than others.

4 Cut 100 mm of beading wire, thread it through the 12 knotted strands, then coil both ends of

the wire around the knot to secure. Apply a drop of fast-drying glue to the knot.

5 Allow the glue to dry completely and trim one end of the wire and the excess tails of beading nylon.

6 Thread the other end of the beading wire through a bead cone and finish with a closed wrapped loop. Trim excess wire.

7 Repeat steps 5 and 6 attaching a bead cone on the other end.

8 Attach a jump ring to one end and the clasp to the other end.

* Variation

An alternative crochet thread can be any thin yarn. Upholstery thread works well, but be prepared to crochet many more strands to get a full effect as regular thread simply does not spring up in the same way as the beading nylon.

Venetian-glass bracelet

Materials and tools

2 x 14 mm round Venetian glass beads (colour 1)

3 x 20 mm Venetian glass rectangles (colour 2)

6 x 8 mm doughnut-shaped crystals (colour 2)

6 x 10 mm silver spacers

8 x 4,5 mm daisy spacers

2 x 4 mm bicone shaped crystals (colour 1)

250 mm flexible beading wire

1 x 12 mm toggle clasp

2 x 10 mm lengths of French wire (optional)

2 crimps

Side cutters

Crimping tool

Approximate length 19,5 cm

Venetian glass beads are so beautiful that the simplest designs show them off best. Austrian crystals in Golden Shadow are the perfect foil for the unusual coral red Venetian beads used in this bracelet. When using large beads you need to allow a little more length to compensate for the bulkiness of the beads.

1 String the following beads onto the flexible beading wire in the order listed below:
  a. 1 crimp bead
  b. 1 x 4 mm bicone crystal (colour 1)
  c. 1 daisy spacer
  d. 1 x 14 mm round Venetian glass bead (colour 1)
  e. 1 daisy spacer
  f. 1 x 8 mm doughnut shaped crystal
  g. 1 x 10 mm silver spacer
  h. 1 x 20 mm venetian glass rectangle (colour 2)
  i. 1 x 10 mm silver spacer
  j. 1 x 8 mm doughnut shaped crystal
  k. repeat b to j twice

2 End with a daisy spacer followed by a 14 mm Venetian round, another daisy spacer and a 4 mm bicone (colour 1).

3 Finish the ends with French wire (optional) and crimp the two parts of the toggle clasp into place.

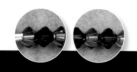

Necklace with detachable pendant

Materials and tools

1 x 6 mm perfect ring
4 head pins
2 crimps
10 mm trigger clasp with ring
2 x 10 mm French wire
12 mm silver toggle clasp
300 mm beading wire, 0,6mm
600 mm flexible beading wire
250 mm flexible beading wire
4 x 4,5 mm daisy spacer
1 x 8 mm silver bead cap
1 x 14 mm round Venetian
  glass bead
1 x 10 mm silver spacer
1 x 8 mm round crystal
  (colour 2)
1 x 6 mm round silver bead
2 x 6 mm round crystals
  (colour 1)
1 x 6 mm silver daisy spacer
2 x doughnut shaped crystals
  (colour 2)
2 x 8 mm silver bead caps
1 x cosmic shaped crystal
  (colour 2)
1 x filigree flower bead link
1 square silver bead
1 x 12 mm crystal drop
63 x 4 mm crystal bicones
  (colour 1)
62 x 4 mm crystal bicones
  (colour 2)
Side cutter

Round-nose pliers
Flat-nose pliers
Chain-nose pliers
Crimping tool

This neckpiece can be worn in two different ways: wear the crystal strand necklace with the toggle clasp to the front and attach the cluster of charms with the trigger clasp for a statement piece. Alternatively, wear it as a simple strand of crystals with the toggle clasp to the back. I strung Austrian crystal bicones in Indian Red and Golden Shadow for a warm effect, matching the striking Venetian glass bead in the pendant. The colours were repeated in the other crystals, offset by oxidised sterling silver findings.

1 Use three head pins and make the following beaded charms for the pendant, ending in wrapped loops:
  a. 1 x 6 mm round crystal (colour 1); 1 x 6 mm silver daisy spacer; 1 x doughnut shaped crystal (colour 2); 1 x 8 mm silver bead cap; 1 x 4 mm bicone (colour 1) (2 in total required)
  b. 1 x 8 mm round crystal (colour 2); 1 x 6 mm round silver bead; 1 x 6 mm round crystal
  c. 1 x 4,5 mm daisy spacer; 1 x 8 mm silver bead cap; 1 x 14 mm round Venetian glass bead; 1 x 10 mm silver spacer; doughnut shaped crystal (colour 2); 1 x daisy spacer.

Approximate length 45 cm excluding pendant

2 Use the fourth headpin to create a beaded charm with 1 x daisy spacer; 1 x cosmic shape crystal (colour 2); 1 x daisy spacer; 1 x 4 mm bicone crystal (colour 1), ending in a common loop linking the filigree flower bead.

3 Use the 250 mm flexible beading wire to attach the 12 mm crystal drop, then add 1 x square silver bead, 1 x 6 mm bicone bead (colour 1) and 1 x crimp bead and make a loop to create a beaded charm (see basic techniques page 33).

4 Use the 0,6 mm beading wire to make five figure of eight loops (see basic techniques page 34). Use the chain-nose pliers and attach the beaded charms to the perfect ring with the figure of eight loops in the order shown in the photograph. Attach the trigger clasp to the perfect ring.

5 Thread the remaining 4 mm crystals onto the long length of flexible beading wire alternating the two colours starting and ending with colour 2 and a crimp bead (approximate length of string 440 mm). Finish with French wire and crimp the two ends of the toggle clasp into place.

6 Attach the charm pendant to the strung crystals.

Crystal and metal choker

Materials and tools

1½ coils of 8 mm
   copper-core silver-plated
   beading wire
   (a hoop of about 480 mm)
2g 6° Japanese seed beads
2 tube crimps (or small balls
   for a neat finish)
4 x 4,5 mm daisy spacers
4 x 10 mm hollow nugget
   shaped metal beads
5 x 8 mm round crystals
6 x 6 mm round crystals
6 x 6 mm crystal bicones
8 head pins
290 mm fine chain
   (3,5 mm links)
2 memory wire ends
   (optional)
Epoxy glue set
Side cutters
Round-nose pliers

Approximate length 42 cm

TIP

Don't be tempted to thread your seed beads by taking the tip of the hoop to your beads as this may kink the wire. Rather feed the beads individually to the hoop in this case.

Metal beads combine well with crystals for an interesting sparkle variation. In this unusual choker, the crystals on sections of chain provide movement in what could easily have been a rather stiff arrangement. All the metal beads, chain and spacers I used are sterling silver. I combined them with Austrian crystals in light Peach Satin, and gold-lined Japanese seed beads in Black Diamond. Do not straighten the coils of beading wire as the hoop must keep its round shape without kinking. When determining the exact size of wire coil to use, you should be able to fit the hoop around your neck with the ends crossing each other by about 10 mm so that it cannot fall off.

1 Divide the chain into the following lengths: 2 x 45 mm, 2 x 40 mm, 4 x 30 mm.

2 Thread 4 x 6 mm round crystals and 4 bicones onto the 8 headpins, finishing in common loops to create charms.

3 Attach the charms to the chains as follows by opening the loop, slipping it over the chain and closing it again: 6 mm round crystals to the 2 x 45 mm chains and 2 x 30 mm chains; bicones to the 2 x 40 mm chains and 2 x 30 mm chains.

4 Thread an 8 mm round crystal onto the wire, positioning it in the centre. Working from both ends, now thread one of the following on each side of the centre bead:

a. 45 mm chain with 6 mm round crystal
b. 10 mm hollow nugget shaped metal bead
c. 40 mm chain with bicone
d. 8 mm round crystals
e. 30 mm chain with 6 mm round crystal
f. 10 mm hollow nugget shaped metal bead
g. 30 mm chain with a bicone
h. 8 mm round crystal
i. 4,5 mm daisy spacer
j. 6 mm round crystal
k. 4,5 mm daisy spacer
l. 6 mm bicone
m. tube crimp

5 Fill the remaining wire on each side with seed beads for an approximate length of 140 mm.

6 Try on for size as different beads may weight the choker differently. Add or remove seed beads until you are satisfied that it is holding correctly, then trim excess wire.

7 Mix the epoxy glue. Working one side at a time, glue a memory-wire end to each end of the hoop and allow to dry thoroughly. If you could not find memory-wire ends, make a neat loop in the wire at each end to stop the seed beads slipping off.

Variation

If you prefer you can attach a clasp. Make a common loop at both ends of the hoop and attach an S-clasp at one end with a ring on the opposite end for it to hook into.

Chandelier earrings

Chandelier earrings will work well with the crystal and metal choker as you can echo the dangling chains on the choker. When assembling earrings like this, decide whether you want the dangling chains to be exactly the same, or a mirror image, and attach them accordingly.

Materials and tools

1 set 2-to-1 chandelier
    earring components
6 x 6 mm crystal bicones
4 x 6 mm round crystals
2 earring posts
    (decorative)
4 head pins
6 eye pins
60 mm chain divided into
    2 x 20 mm and
    2 x 10 mm

1 Use the head pins to create charms with four of the bicones, ending in common loops and attach them to the four lengths of chain.

2 Use the eye pins to create double-ended beaded loops with all the remaining crystals.

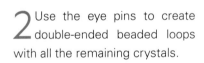

3 Attach the 4 round crystals to the unadorned ends of the chains then attach them to the double ends of the chandelier earring components.

4 Attach the last two double-ended crystal bicones to the single end of the chandelier earring components and then to the loop of each earring post.

✳ Variation

Using the same technique, these earrings are slightly more elaborate and have been made with sterling silver and facetted garnets

TIP

If your chandelier earring component has more than two ends, adjust the design to hang more beaded chain strands of varying lengths.

Multi-strand wire choker

Materials and tools

3 x 550 mm strands flexible beading wire (colours 1, 2, 3)

4 x 8 mm facetted gemstone beads (colour 1)

3 x 8 mm facetted gemstone beads (colour 2)

1 x 8 mm Czech fire-polished bead (colour 2 clear)

2 x 8 mm Czech fire-polished beads (colour 3)

2 x 6 mm Czech fire-polished beads (colour 3)

45 mm chain (3 mm oval links) in 1 x 30 mm and 1 x 15 mm sections

6 head pins

20 mm x 0,6 mm silver-plated wire for figure of 8 loop)

1 x 4,5 mm daisy spacer (oxidised)

4 x 2 mm tube crimps

4 x 3 mm crimp covers

1 x 1 mm trigger clasp

Side cutters

Crimping tool

Round-nose pliers

This very simple design uses flexible beading wire or tigertail which is available in many colours, so why not use it as a design feature. Here I used flexible beading wire in the same three colours as the gemstones: silver, black and dark pink. I used facetted gemstones, namely hematite and rhodonite, Czech fire-polished beads in black (Jet) and Antique Rose with sterling silver chain and spacers.

1 Use the head pins to create six charms with the following beads, ending with common loops:

   a. 1 x daisy spacer and 1 x 8 mm facetted gemstone bead in colour 2

   b. 2 x 6 mm Czech fire-polished beads (colour 3)

   c. 2 x 8 mm facetted gemstone beads (colour 1)

   d. 1 x 8 mm Czech fire-polished bead (colour 2 clear).

2 Attach these charms to the longer length of chain at three-link intervals in the following order: 1 x a, 1 x b, 1 x c, 1 x b.

3 Attach the remaining c to the end of the shorter chain and d six links up, then link the two chains at the top with a figure of eight loop.

4 Put together the three strands of wire and thread on the following, positioning everything at the centre of the combined strands of wire:

   a. 1 crimp

   b. 1 x 8 mm Czech fire-polished bead (colour 3)

   c. 1 x 8 mm facetted gemstone beads (colour 1)

   d. 1 x 8 mm facetted gemstone bead (colour 2)

   e. the linked chains

   f. 1 x 8 mm facetted gemstone bead (colour 2)

g. 1 x 8 mm facetted gemstone bead (colour 1)

h. 1 x 8 mm Czech fire-polished bead (colour 3)

i. 1 crimp

5 Check the positioning to ensure that the beads are centred, secure in position using the folded crimp technique and cover with crimp covers (see basic techniques page 38)

TIP

When crimping multiple strands of wire make sure they are not crossed over in the crimp. Try to get them to lie neatly next to one another before squashing the crimp into place.

6 Measure 190 mm from the covered crimp to the end of the wires, add a crimp, thread back into the loop one of the strands of wire to form a loop and squash the crimp exactly at the 190 mm mark. Cut the excess wire as close to the crimp as possible and add a crimp cover to finish neatly.

7 Repeat on the other side but thread the loop wire through the clasp before crimping, securing and trimming. Add a crimp cover to finish neatly.

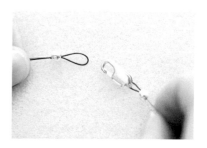

Approximate length 40 cm excluding drop

Brittle-tooth pearl bracelet

Materials and tools

24 top-drilled brittle-tooth
pearls (colour 1)
11 x 5/6 mm round crystals
(colour 1)
48 x 4 mm crystal bicones
(colour 2)
1 antique brass magnetic
multi-strand clasp
60 mm length of flexible
beading wire (colour 2)
2 crimps (to match clasp)
Side cutters
Crimping tool

The irregular shapes of top-drilled brittle-tooth pearls offer lots of scope for creativity and I designed this cuff bracelet to look like a garland of flowers. I used a bright fuchsia pearl with a slightly more subdued 8 mm round Austrian crystal in Rose Satin, beautifully offset by the 4 mm crystal bicones in striking tourmaline.

1 Thread the flexible beading wire through the two outer holes in the multi-strand magnetic clasp (if this is too wide, use the next two holes) and pull down so that you have two tails of equal length.

2 Thread the following beads onto each tail:
   a. 2 x 4 mm bicones
   b. 2 pearls
   c. 2 x 4 mm crystal bicones

3 Thread a 6 mm round crystal onto one tail only, then take the other tail through the same round from the other side (in other wordS, the tails are crossed over in the crystal).

4 Continue with the pattern as follows:
   a. 2 x 4 mm crystal bicones onto each tail
   b. 2 pearls onto each tail
   c. 2 x 4 mm crystal bicones onto each tail

5 Thread a 6 mm round crystal onto one tail only, then take the other tail through the same round from the other side crossing the tails over in the crystal.

6 Repeat this sequence until all the pearls have been used.

7 Add a 4 mm bicone and a crimp bead to both tails, thread the wire through the two outer holes of the clasp and back through the crimp and a crystal on the other side.

TIP
As this is a tight-fitting bracelet, measure it before crimping so that you can still make adjustments without having to restring everything.

8 Pull both strands tight in opposite directions so that the beads sit snug against the clasp and squash the crimps to secure (see basic techniques page 36).

9 Trim the wire as close to the beads as possible.

Beaded cocktail rings

Materials and tools

4 x 8 mm round Venetian
  glass beads
6 x 6 mm Czech pressed-
  glass tiles
6 x 8 mm round crystals
16 silver headpins
1 beaded ring-base with
  8 loops
Side cutters
Chain-nose pliers
Round-nose pliers

These rings are great fun to make and will never have a neutral reception! They have wonderful movement and can really be worn with flair. I used chartreuse coloured Venetian glass beads with Czech pressed glass tiles in a similar colour and Austrian crystals in lime on a solid silver beaded ring-base.

1 Use the head pins to create charms with all the beads, ending in common loops (see basic techniques page 25).

2 Use the chain nose pliers and randomly attach two charms to each loop of the ring by opening linking and closing the common loops.

TIP

Take care not to link similar beads in close proximity to each other so that the ring is well balanced.

* Variation

Vary the shape, colour and size of the beads to suit your taste. For this variation I used Czech pressed-glass flowers and leaves with 6 mm Austrian crystals in pink alabaster to create a soft, feminine look.

Necklace with briolette clusters

Materials and tools

1 x 14 mm round Venetian
glass bead (or other
matching focal bead)
10 x 8 mm round crystals
(colour 1)
6 x 8 mm round crystals
(colour 2)
3 x 6 mm round crystals
(colour 1)
9 x 4,5 mm daisy spacers
22 x 10 mm gemstone
briolettes (top-drilled drops)
19 x 4 mm crystal bicones
(colour 3)
2 x 5 mm spring spacers
1 head pin
2 x 10 mm lengths of French
wire (optional)
2 crimps
50 x 8° Japanese seed beads
(match colour of drops)
600 mm flexible beading wire
60 mm chain
(4 or 5 mm links)
1 x 10 mm trigger clasp
Side cutters
Crimping Tool
Round-nose pliers

Approximate length 45 cm

Drop-shaped beads, or briolettes, are top drilled and often pose a challenge in design. I used their shape as a feature in this piece with the beads lying opposite one another creating flower-like clusters with simple stringing. Here I used rose quarts briolettes with Austrian crystals in Vintage Rose, light Peach Satin and Golden Shadow. The Venetian glass focal bead is soft salmon pink.

1 Group the briolettes to size as follows: 6 x 3 and 2 x 2 beads. Thread them with the largest towards the centre of the necklace with the smallest towards the back.

2 Thread the focal bead onto the flexible beading wire and take it to the centre.

3 Thread the following beads on both tails on either side of the focal bead:

a. 1 x 5 mm spring spacer
b. 1 x 8 mm round crystal (col 1)
c. 1 x 4 mm bicone
d. 3 largest briolettes opposite one another
e. 1 x 4 mm bicone
f. 1 x 8 mm round crystal (col 1)
g. 1 x 4,5 mm daisy spacer
h. 1 x 8 mm round crystal (col 2)
i. 1 x 4 mm bicone crystal
j. 3 second largest briolettes opposite one another
k. Repeat steps e to j, then repeat e to i once more

l. 2 smallest briolettes opposite one another
m. 1 x 4 mm bicone
n. 1 x 8 mm round crystal (col 1)
o. 1 daisy spacer
p. 1 x 6 mm round crystal (col 2)
q. 1 x 8° seed bead
r. 1 x 4 mm bicone

4 Continue threading 8° seed beads until the beaded string measures 440 mm.

5 Finish the ends with French wire (optional). Loop crimp one end to the ring of the trigger clasp and attach the extension chain to the other end.

6 Thread the following beads on the head pin to make a beaded charm for the extension chain:
a. 1 x 6 mm round crystal
b. 1 daisy spacer
c. 1 x 4 mm biconel

7 End with a common loop and attach to the end of the extension chain.

Clustered tassel pendant

Materials and tools

1 large gemstone rectangle
  (focal bead gem 1)
14 x 6 mm round crystals
  (colour 1)
13 x 6 mm round crystals
  (colour 2)
23 x 4 mm round Czech
  fire-polished beads
  (colour 3)
6 x 8 mm doughnut shaped
  crystals (colour 2)
19 x 6 mm round gemstones
  (gem 1)
35 small gemstone chips
  (gem 2)
12 freshwater pearls (colour
  1)
10 x 6 mm silver bead caps
6 x 8 mm flat oval gemstones
  (gem 1)
90 mm chain (3,5 mm oval
  links) in 1 x 60 mm and 1 x
  30 mm sections
2 crimps
1 x 30 mm decorative S-clasp
25 x 4,5 mm daisy spacers
2 x 10 mm lengths French
  wire (optional)
70 head pins
60 cm flexible beading wire

300 mm silver or silver-plated
  beading wire, 0,6 mm (or thick
  enough to go through hole in
  focal bead)
30 mm silver chain
  (3,5 mm oval links)
Side cutters
Round-nose pliers
Chain-nose pliers
Crimping tool

If someone had to ask me what my signature style is, this would be a firm favourite. This technique allows much creative freedom and is a way of making chunky pieces out of small beads. Here I used a combination of carnelian and turquoise gemstones with matching freshwater pearls and Austrian crystals in Sun Satin and Erinite. The Czech fire-polished beads are green lustre. All findings and spacer beads are oxidised sterling silver.

1 Use the 0,6 mm beading wire and create a double-ended wrapped loop with the focal bead, linking the 30 mm chain to the bottom end and finishing the top with a daisy spacer before making the wrapped loop (see basic techniques page 27).

2 Use the head pins to create charms with the following beads, ending in common loops (see basic techniques page 25):

a. 22 gemstone chips
b. 8 pearls
c. 14 x 4 mm fire polished beads
d. 14 x 6 mm round gemstones
  (gem 1)
e. 8 x 6 mm round crystals
  (colour 2)
f. 1 daisy spacer and 1 x 6 mm
  round crystal (colour 2)
g. 1 daisy spacer and 1 x 6 mm
  round crystal (colour 1)
h. 1 x 6 mm round crystal
  (colour 1)
i. 1 daisy spacer, 1 x 6 mm
  round gemstone, 1 gemstone
  chip, 1 x 4 mm fire-polished
  bead (this will be the detail
  drop at the end of the extension chain)

TIP

If some of your beads seem to get too tucked away and you feel they need to stand out a little, add three or four matching seed beads when making the charms on the head pins before closing the loops. This will allow the bead to stand out.

3 Thread the prepared focal bead onto the flexible beading wire and centre it on the wire. Thread one of each of the following beads onto both sides of the pendant:

a. 1 daisy spacer
b. 6 mm round crystal (colour 1)
c. Bead cap (small side first)
d. 8 mm round doughnut shaped crystal (colour 2)

4 Now thread the following charms and beads one each onto both sides:

a. 1 gemstone chip charm
b. 1 x 6 mm round gemstone charm
c. 1 x 5 mm round fire-polished charm
d. 1 x 6 mm round crystal (colour 1)
e. 1 gemstone chip charm
f. 1 pearl charm
g. 1 x 6 mm round crystal (colour 2) charm

h. 1 x 5 mm round fire-polished bead
i. 1 x 6 mm round gemstone charm
j. 1 x gemstone chip charm
k. 1 x looped 5mm round fire-polished charm
l. 1 x daisy spacer
m. 1 x 8 mm oval gemstone bead

5 Repeat steps 3 and 5 two more times on both sides. You should have three sets of these beaded groups on either side of the focal bead.

6 Thread the remaining beads onto both sides as follows:

a. 1 daisy spacer
b. 1 x 6 mm round crystal (colour 1)
c. 1 x bead cap (small side first)

d. 1 x 6 mm round crystal (colour 2)
e. 1 daisy spacer
f. 1 pearl
g. 3 gemstone chips
h. 1 x daisy spacer
i. 1 x 6 mm round gemstone
j. Repeat c to i
k. 1 x 5 mm fire polished bead
l. Crimp bead.

7 Finish one end by threading the French wire and attaching the clasp, crmping it to secure (see basic techniques page 00), and make a loop at the other end with the French wire (see basic techniques page 00), at the same time attaching the extension chain.

8 Attach the drop made in step 2i to the end of the extension chain.

9 Attach the remaining charms to the chain on the focal bead. Place them randomly, holding up the chain vertically to find the gaps.

Variation

I often do not use a focal bead when using this design template, but simply link the chain tassel onto the centre of the wire for a softer look. In this variation of the basic cluster design I used faceted aquamarine gemstones, freshwater pearls, Swarovski crystals in Ceylon AB, light Azure and light Colorado Topaz.

Approximate length 45 cm excluding extension chain and drop

Be Inspired to Make Beautiful Jewelry!

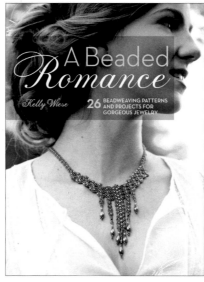

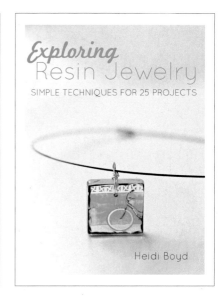

The Beaded Bracelet
Beadweaving Techniques &
Patterns for 20 Eye-Catching
Projects
Carole Rodgers

SRN: X9675
ISBN10: 144031277X

A Beaded Romance
26 Beadweaving Patterns and
Projects for Gorgeous Jewelry
Kelly Wiese

SRN: V8199
ISBN13: 9781440232138

Exploring Resin Jewelry
Simple Techniques for 25 Projects
Heidi Boyd

SRN: W6552
ISBN13: 9781440318726

Check out BeadingDaily.com—our vibrant, online beading community where you'll find free beading projects, free beading stitch and jewelry making tutorials, expert advice and information about the latest trends in beading and jewelry making.